God bless you
as you seek His will

Ken Smith 2/11/09

Inupiat Parables

Ken Smith

iUniverse, Inc.
New York   Bloomington

Inupiat Parables

iUniverse books may be ordered through booksellers or by contacting:

iUniverse
1663 Liberty Drive
Bloomington, IN 47403
www.iuniverse.com
1-800-Authors (1-800-288-4677)

Because of the dynamic nature of the Internet, any Web addresses or
links contained in this book may have changed since publication and
may no longer be valid. The views expressed in this work are solely those
of the author and do not necessarily reflect the views of the publisher,
and the publisher hereby disclaims any responsibility for them.

ISBN: 978-1-4401-1310-9 (pbk)
ISBN: 978-1-4401-1311-6 (ebk)

Printed in the United States of America

iUniverse rev. date: 1/12/2009

INTRODUCTION

To GET TO THE COMMUNITY of Wainwright you fly from Seattle to Anchorage, then from Anchorage to Fairbanks and from Fairbanks to Barrow. Then you transfer to a smaller plane, continue west about a hundred miles to Wainwright and when you land you change the name to Olgoonik, which is the Inupiat name for the city.

There are two varieties of Eskimo folk. The northern Inupiat Eskimo folk are those who live on the North Slope, that geographical area between the Brooks Range and the Arctic Ocean. The Yup'ik folk live in Western Alaska and often have close relatives in Eastern Siberia. The word Inupiat means "the people" in the Inupiat language.

Wainwright, though it has stood on the present spot, between Wainwright Inlet and the Chukchi Sea for centuries, inhabited by about 500 folk, was named in 1826 by British Captain F. W. Beechly for his officer Lt. John Wainwright.

The word Olgoonik is the Inupiat word for a place where the sod homes of early Eskimos built on the cliff above the sea fell into the ocean during a great storm that eroded the bluff. The beaches are continuing to erode but more of that later.

You are now in an Inupiat town where there is no private enterprise. Instead the city fathers, village leaders and their corporation own all enterprise. There is a single internet connection at the Walrus Cafe and you wait your turn to use it. If there are several who wish to use it, relax, it will be a long wait. When you buy anything in the Walrus Café, you do not need change for all prices are in even dollars. It is very tasty "white man" (tunik) food served by waiters and waitresses who are interested not only in what you eat, but who you are.

There is a modern water system, with the water stored in those tanks over there. The sewer system is modern and both the water and sewer systems are built with insulated piping so nothing freezes. You may smell some different smells, especially if someone has just butchered a walrus and the stomach contents have been exposed.

Your transportation around town probably will be by All Terrain Vehicles, one or two-person vehicles with large tires made for travel over difficult terrain during the summer or by Snow Machine, with a single rubber track that propels you over ice or snow during the winter. Gasoline and heating oil come in once a year by barge. If you must move or carry something large there are trucks in town, but most people just walk for the town extends about a mile from one end to the other and is bordered by tundra at both ends, by the Chukchi sea to the North and a lake to the South.

There is a sense of isolation when the weather turns sour or the fog comes in off the sea or the ice bergs drift by. However, from Olgoonik you can travel to any and everyplace else in the world, although the residents prefer to stay in Olgoonik. Gene and Jean Straatmeyer and grand daughter Layni spent a month on a preaching mission in Olgoonik. Gene had served the Inupiat folk in the Fairbanks area so was familiar with cultural mores and family ties. These parables are partly a result of Gene's observations. The Olgoonik church is served by Commissioned Lay Pastor George Agnassagga and his wife Lydia.

A parable is an earthly story or event with a heavenly meaning. Jesus was not the first to use parables in his teaching. Scripture is filled with many examples of parabolic teaching but the parables really contain some of Jesus Christ's deepest theology.

Contemplate and enjoy!

Contents

ESKIMO LABOR

"Then I realized that it is good and proper for a man to eat and
drink, and to find satisfaction in his toilsome labor under the sun
during the few days of life God has given him-for this is his lot.
Morever, when God gives any man wealth and possessions, and
enables him to enjoy them, to accept his lot and be happy in his
work-this is a gift of God. He seldom reflects on the days of his
life, because God keeps him occupied with gladness of heart.
Ecclesiastes 5:18-20

THE TSA CHECKER WENT THROUGH the belongings and when he came upon
a tube of toothpaste he removed it. "But," the owner said, "I went through
two other check points and they did not take it." The reply with a smile was,
"We are just doing our job - the others weren't"

The Eskimo folk of the northern part of Alaska are known for doing
just what their job happens to be. When faced with extremes of weather and
survival conditions, doing a complete job is sometimes the difference between
life and death. When the seams of a skin are to be stretched over a frame
to create a whale boat, every seam must be watertight. To leave a few seams
less than perfect, can sink the boat when the excitement of a whale hunt is
under way.

Sometimes this means that a job is not started because the person
supposedly doing the job does not feel that he or she can complete the
activity. The tanik (white man) may blame the worker with laziness, or just
plain stubbornness but the worker realizes that to do part of a job without
completion is to do nothing at all. It is better for someone else to do the
activity than to be related to something that is less than the best.

The Inupiat folk have wonderful abilities. They don't have a long history of
working with engines, but many of them can take apart an engine, fix what
is not working, and put it back together again. That is often necessary if there
is a major breakdown while out on a trail with nothing but snow around.

There is a similarity between the Eskimo worker and a person who makes
a commitment to the Christian faith, a stated belief that Jesus the Christ is
the son of God and that his death has a new and wonderful meaning for the

person making the statement. The commitment is not only in words alone but also in his commitment to serving in the church, sharing with his neighbor of tangible assets, the purity of his language and singing of songs of praise to God.

Each of us needs to realize that when we make a confession to be Christlike (Christian) that, at the same time, we are growing. Some fear making such a commitment because of all that it can entail. We do not make that commitment when we consider ourselves perfect, but when we are ready to follow Jesus and his teachings.

The more we study the word of God, the more we realize what following Jesus is all about. It is better if we accept the position of being a new, young, Christian where all of our Christian life will be a time of growing, physically and also spiritually even to old age.

God's word will seem new to the person who honestly examines it in relation to his or her own life. As there are spurts in our physical growth, from childhood to old age, so there are spurts in our spiritual growth. There are concepts that Jesus brought to view, occasionally to explain those things that happened in the Old Testament, that help us to grow first as children and then on through our mature life until we reach old age.

We need to remember that the gift of eternal life is not earned by being perfect, but that we strive to be perfect because we have been given that gift of eternal life. There are many other religious beliefs that state that you have to be perfect to come before God, or the creator, but God does not expect that. Rather he expects that the "intent"to follow Jesus's teachings is there.

God sees and knows the intention of our hearts and it is his determination that he would like to spend the rest of eternity with us. We do make mistakes, but when we are honest and admit them to God he realizes that we are in the growth process and that the process continues on through our lives.

At the same time you are growing, your family and friends also will realize how much change takes place when you do your best to follow Jesus' teachings, his way of dealing with others and his intense show of love to each one of us and to the world. He loves each individual with a self-giving love, and that is the way that we should show our love to others. We should not take something from them, but give as much as we can in honest concern for their lives.

When we finally mature, we can then realize that our job is not to judge others as to their growth, their witness or how they live their lives, but rather it is our business to look at ourselves and show that we have been with Jesus during our lives. Yes, we can note the facts of others' lives and point out to our children those things that will not be in God's will, but that becomes a matter of learning.

The Book of Proverbs in the Bible lists things that help us to guide our lives. They have been successful for thousands of years and a slow reading of the proverbs now gives us a "before-Jesus" view of how to raise our children, and how to act in life to be successfully related to God.

"Loving God, we long to be in your presence, to feel the warmth of your love and to live the lives that you would have us live. Guide us as we grow not only older but also closer to you. In Jesus's name we pray. Amen."

EVEN THE WHALES OBEY

"Then God said, 'Let us make man in our image, in our likeness, and
let them rule over the fish of the sea and the birds of the air, over the
livestock, over all the earth, and over all the creatures that move along
the ground.' So God created man in his own image, in the image of
God he created him; male and female he created them. God blessed
them and said to them, 'Be fruitful and increase in number; fill the
earth and subdue it. Rule over the fish of the sea and the birds of
the air and over every living creature that moves on the ground.'"
Genesis 1:26-28

THE INUPIAT ELDER WAS EXPLAINING to the young tanic girl how the Eskimo
hunters went out on the ocean for whales, how they would take their boats
over the solid ice to where the water began. There they would launch their
boats and begin to hunt for the whales. When one was spotted they would
get close and harpoon the whale, and when it had died it would be pulled
through the water to the solid ice and from there it would be dragged over
the ice to the village.

Then he said, "We have a belief that God instructs some whales to give
their lives for the Inupiat so they can eat. It is a phenomenon that happens
every season. Several whales will swim right alongside the boat for easy
harpooning and certain death." Her eyes were wide with amazement, but he
said that it had happened often.

He continued, "When the meat is given to the village, for all share in
the feast, there is a blessing when we give thanks to God. We often have the
same feeling, of God giving us food when hunting for other animals in the
water or on land, when just at the right moment the animal appears and the
hunter is successful."

There are probably few who would like to use the food staples that the
Inupiat uses. Whale meat, along with other arctic Eskimo food sources, is
very oily. For the Eskimo folk to survive, however the oil that they consume
is necessary to help insulate them from the extreme cold that they experienced
almost the entire year.

Other food providers, hunters, farmers often have the same feeling as they go about the business of gathering food for communities. It seems as though God is leading them to places and situations that provide food which normally would not exist. Too often they see this as a 'lucky break' or the 'toss of the coin' and do not give the credit to God who provides for each and all of us.

We are entering a time of high cost food where the swelling population of the world requires almost more food that we can supply, either agricultural or from the sea. The Inupiat are excellent stewards for the entire animal is used either for food or for clothing, or possibly to make artifacts that can be sold to tourists.

Their food does not allow them to become large folk and that is good for they must spend much time in very warm suits. We found that at Sheldon Jackson Junior College in Sitka, and at Mt. Edgecumbe school that also served the arctic villages. There was plenty of nutritious food, supplied in the school by the taniks, and the youth from the arctic slope often grew three or four inches in height during the school year.

God is the source of all that we have and are. The blessing that is said before each meal is an acknowledgment that God has provided the food, even though at the hands of other folks, and so we thank him for what we have. There is always the joke about the fact that we have doubly blessed food as it was blessed the first time and now we are eating the leftovers.

In God's creation he made the soil regenerative so that after a rest it is again capable of growing the food that will enable human life to survive. As he rested on the seventh day, so do the farmers give their fields a chance to rest. At other times they grow a crop that will be turned back into the soil from which it came, to re-enervate and restore the fertility of the soil.

Possibly we can learn from both the farmers and God that it is wise for us to make and take a day of rest, a time when normal work activities can be laid aside. We can spend the time either in resting or growing mentally and spiritually to be new people at the beginning of our next time of labor. The Eskimo hunter rests often before the excitement of the hunt.

Worship services are planned to give the participant an opportunity to rest. In our lives, we too often emphasize sports and other activities that really are not resting at all. The value of a rest, or even a nap, has been recognized by industry where the executives and workers often are given a time of rest during the day. Management realizes that rest creates an opportunity for a better worker time in the afternoon. Decisions made and labor accomplished proves this.

In spite of the demand placed upon our food sources, a time of rest is going to be a necessity in order to provide all the food that the world demands. It is still God who provides the food,

God provides the whales for the Inupiat hunter, and also provides all that we have and are.

Realizing that the land was necessary, the Presbyterian Church has morally supported and financially aided the Inupiat folk, to secure the land and resources that they use in their daily life. Where other interests would like to take the land, and all profits from the use of it, such as drilling for oil, the Presbyterian church made funds available to the North Slope Borough so that they could operate during their first year. These funds have been repaid to the church, but the fact remains that the church has supported the people of the Borough in their struggle to be self-supporting. God still provides through Christian people the means for others to come to him.

There is a greater lesson in this parable. God provided the whales for the Inupiat folk to have food. God also provided his Son, Jesus the Christ, whose death on a cross and resurrection provide not only a means of coming to God through faith, but also as a means to grow and live a life that is peaceful and pleasant where all mankind can live together. This is provided so that we can honor and glorify God and those who accept Christ as God's son, show honor to God.

"Father God, we thank you for the provisions that you make for us. We thank you for Christian folks who assist us not only in our growth but also in our maintenance. May we recognize others who are in need and to the best of our ability assist them in their needs. Particularly, though Father God, we thank you for your son, Jesus the Christ, for his life and death and resurrection and for the blending together of all his people, those who accept personally that death and resurrection. May we live as honest witnesses to your love. In Jesus's name we pray. Amen."

PLANES WITH SHOES

"I warn everyone who hears the words of the prophecy of this book,
if anyone adds anything to them, God will add to him the plagues
described in this book. And if any one takes words away from this
book of prophecy, God will take away from him his share in the
tree of life and in the holy city, which are described in this book."
Revelation 22:18, 19

THERE ARE MANY ACCOMMODATIONS MADE for conditions in Alaska. Planes that are kept in the open overnight in the winter must have their oil drained and then reheated before it is put into the engine, as cold oil will not circulate through the engine. Planes must be equipped with emergency life saving items because occasionally a plane has a malfunction and must land. If it is dark the plane may offer the only shelter for the night. Emergency items include beacons so that those who are searching can find the planes that might have come down in a wooded area.

Most of the remote landing strips in Alaska have gravel runways and taxi strips. Therefore the planes must have "shoes" or rock shields on both wheels that prevent stones and small gravel particles from hitting the tail section of the plane. They are a necessary protection that ensures that the plane can continue flying.

As Christians we also need a protective measure. There are thousands of beliefs in the world, and many of them 'seem' to be very good and also 'seem' to be the same beliefs that we as Christian folk have. However people often become so obsessed with their own denomination's theological stand that they forget that the Bible is our standard rule of faith and practice. Our protective shoes consist of God's word.

Many of the sects and cults of the world just take parts of the Bible to prove their theological consistency. It seems they believe that if they can use the Bible to define some particular stand that they have, then that makes all of their total beliefs acceptable. The protection, the 'shoes' that protect us, are regular and consistent Bible study groups. It is difficult for a minister or lay preacher to cover all kinds of theological beliefs in a twenty minute sermon on a Sunday morning. Therefore a study group that meets regularly, encourages participation by everyone in the congregation and focuses on the Bible, not a secular book, can be a strong instrument in the Christian Education of the congregation.

Such a study group can begin with the life of Christ, using a harmony of the gospels which contains the accounts of the New Testament times showing the parallel versions of Matthew, Mark, Luke and John. The consistency of God's Word can be illustrated by following the life of Christ, from his birth to his death and resurrection in the gospels.

Some ministers use the study groups to encourage comments from the lay folk and often incorporate those ideas, questions or comments in the next Sunday's sermon. Many lay folk grow when they realize that they have helped illustrate some point that the minister is making the following Sunday. Some pastors or Commissioned Lay Pastors invite the congregation to suggest sermons that they would like to hear, concerning subjects pertinent to the secular world in which they are living.

Also important in providing "protection shoes" is a church library that caters to the theological and Bible study using Bible dictionaries, commentaries, concordances and other source books for individual study. In our daily lives we are going to encounter many differing beliefs, but they are not binding for the Christian believer and a library that has not only inspirational books but also Bible Study materials is a great asset. The growing pastor needs to do regular study and he or she should encourage the members of the congregation to take part in that educational and spiritual growth as well.

Often the members of a congregation will encounter some individual who has studied, from their own denomination's viewpoint, some passage of scripture. The member may feel weak in his defense of what the Bible says. Bible Studies should honestly encounter all the various points of theology and Biblical knowledge and provide a satisfactory answer to questions posed by members of other denominations and sects.

Sunday School is a wonderful means of Christian Education, but if an individual comes to the Christian faith later in life there is much knowledge that he or she does not have. It is very helpful for such a person to read a Bible Story book that tells the various stories that are associated with the time line of the Christian faith, reading the stories of the Old Testament heros first and then reading about the life of Christ. This is particularly helpful if the pastor realizes that there are persons who have little Bible knowledge, and therefore it helps them to understand various concepts upon which the pastor is speaking. This type of learning is often used in the learning of a new language, where the learner reads children's books and easily increases his knowledge of the language.

If the pastor is reading from a manuscript it is also helpful to have copies of that manuscript available for the members of the congregation at the end of the service. Also helpful in educating the congregation are tapes that were taken during the regular worship service and that can be listened to during the following week at the congregant's leisure.

Pastors welcome questions and comments from members of the congregation, and often the pastor who is well read can suggest particular books that help the new member or reader to understand points of view that they have not encountered previously.

Church libraries are also helpful in educating and interesting children in the Bible and these books can be helpful to others. Often adult members of the congregation will use the children's books to clarify some particular problem, and they should be encouraged to do so. Remember, the pilot of a plane never knows when he is going to encounter gravel that can damage his aircraft. Likewise the pastor of a congregation, speaking to all levels of theological knowledge and maturity every Sunday morning has a difficult time interpreting God's Word to those who may have no prior knowledge of the Bible. He or she also faces the problem of people of maintaining continuity for people who missed church the previous week or week or two particularly if he is preaching a series of sermons.

"Loving Father God, help us as we learn more of your words and your Word. Give us the clarity of understanding about the lives that were lived by your saints, and a deeper understanding of the teachings of Jesus and also the early Church. Give us the ability to teach others and the thrill of bringing wisdom to those around us in the church, in our families, and in the community. Give us clear wisdom that our witness might be honest for you. This we pray in your son's name. Amen."

CELL PHONE SILLINESS CEASES

"For attaining wisdom and discipline; for understanding words
of insight; for acquiring a disciplined and prudent life, doing
what is right and just and fair; for giving prudence to the simple,
knowledge and discretion to the young - let the wise listen and
add to their learning and let the discerning get guidance."
Proverbs 1:2-5

ONE OF THE WONDERFUL THINGS that one appreciates when heading off into the Arctic wilderness is the lack of cell phones. Yes, there is a Citizen's Band which is a means of communication but the silly-ness that has permeated not only our society but the society of folks around the world is the continual use and mis-use of cell phones.

One cannot live a normal life when people use cell phones while driving in automobiles, waiting in stores, in airport waiting rooms, on trains and street cars, in school, and on the playground. You name the place and someone has found that they just 'Have' to use the cell phone to talk to someone. It is strange because just about every use I see of the cell phone involves people talking and somewhere out in the vast space of humanity there are people who are not talking but just listening, doing the dishes, working cross word puzzles, or picture puzzles. Possibly they are in a car where both of the people in the front seat are talking to different persons on cell phones, while the kids in the back seat are trying to get their attention. Of course the kids are told to keep quiet so they do not disturb the cell phone conversation.

And now you can take pictures with your cell phone, or do your business or translate the iPod, or do a host of other things, except paying attention to those with you. We have driven behind persons who were talking on their cell phones, slow to leave a stop sign, or weaving back and forth in their lane so much that you wonder if the problem is the cell phone tightly clasped to their ears, or possibly a misuse of alcohol.

So it is good to get to the Arctic wilderness, for most cell phones will not reach all the corners of the northern Arctic wonderland. Not only that, but most of the batteries will lose their charge in the extreme temperatures encountered in the northern part of Alaska.

It seems that we have become a talking generation, but everyone is talking and no one is listening. We fill our ears with talking and music to the extent that we do not understand God's word, "Be still and know that I am God." Perhaps our use of cell phones results in the prayers that we offer - long petitions that we seldom give God a chance to answer.

Counselors are experiencing couples who come for help with both demanding to be heard. The couple never realize that for both to be heard one of them has to be quiet for part of the time. It is difficult for counselors to gain the import of the problems that the couple are experiencing when both must answer each other so quickly that the counselor has no time to process the encounter and to understand what they are really saying to each other.

The writer of the book of James makes his point about listening in the 19th verse of the first Chapter, "My dear brothers, take note of this: Everyone should be quick to listen, slow to speak and slow to become angry," and he continues in the 22nd verse, "But do not merely listen to the word, and so deceive yourselves. Do what it says."

A successful member of the Arctic society learns how to listen - to the cracking of the ice on which he is traveling, to the hiss of a sea mammal as he or she breaks water, to the wind, and to each other. The quietness of the Arctic actually involves many noises, but they are quieter sounds.

Listening is important in understanding God's word, but James would encourage us not only to listen but to do the Word of God. The book of Proverbs was usually learned by a Jewish youth before he passed his Son of the Covenant examination. If wise, the young man would continue to listen to what God's word had to say to him. In the silence of the eternity in which we are presently in the middle of, God's word to us demands that we listen to what he says. He was, is and will be in charge of our lives, if we are to live productive lives for him.

God's Word is all we need. With quiet understanding we can hear what he wants, desires and expects of us. If we want to face him in eternity, then it is wise for us to develop the listening attitude now while we tread the planet earth. As a deaf person once said, "Now that I am deaf I can listen to God and no one interrupts me. Yes I have time to wonder what others are trying to tell me but ultimately I can remember the music of the world, and I can listen for the God of the word as he speaks to me. I don't need hearing to hear him."

"Gracious God, help us to be still and know that you are God. In the quietness of each day speak to us, not so we miss the voices of others, but first we would hear your voice. Let us listen to others in our times of personal encounter, but ultimately let us listen to your voice and the voices of those who have gone before us. For we pray in Jesus's name. Amen."

WANTED: A PASTOR

"Do not be afraid when some become rich, when the wealth
of their houses increases, for when they die they will carry
nothing away; their wealth will not go down after them
though in their lifetime they count themselves happy."
Psalm 49:16-18

"THE THRIVING METROPOLIS OF OLGOONIK is surrounded by the majestic Blue Ridge Mountains and an abundance of natural beauty. The home to East Tennessee State University Colleges of Medicine and Pharmacy, Olgoonik uniquely blends economic growth opportunities, affordable housing, strong public and private schools, and traditional Southern hospitality to provide an ideal location for raising Christian families.

"Historic downtown First Presbyterian Church seeks a pastor: Minimum of six years preaching/teaching experience with a clear passion for Christ - Biblically-centered sermons delivered with enthusiasm, wit and wisdom. Organizational and management skills, compassionate, outgoing and accessible. Special attention to church growth and young families. Phone 907-763-2415"

Well, if that did not draw some applications, possibly I can use this one:

"Pastor/Head of Staff. Olgoonik is an active thriving congregation of nearly xxx members. Our recently concluded stewardship campaign was our best ever! Through a *Journey for Discernment* we have developed a vision for our future that is full of mission and ministry opportunities. We seek a pastor/head of staff who will help us use that vision to create deeper connections with God, community and world.

"Ideally, our new pastor should have a minimum of 8 years experience as pastor or associate pastor. The pastor must be able to engage us with intellectually stimulating, biblically centered sermons delivered with enthusiasm, humility and a sense of humor.

"Other skills expected include: participating as a teacher in our thriving Christian Education program, offering spiritual guidance to congregation

12

and staff, and working collaboratively with our Associate Pastor to strengthen small group ministries. If you meet these criteria, please send your PIF (Pastor Information Form) to our session. Telephone 907-763-2415."

Possibly that would not work. In case neither of these advertisements work, maybe I should say that, "We want a pastor who cries with us when we cry, laughs with us when we laugh, prays for us, and will help us understand a simple Jesus who showed a deep love for people - not just the city folk who worship in big mobs but also the country folk of Galilee, just the common folk. We don't need one who rants and raves and is going to consign each of us to a permanent hell. He would know more about it than would we. We want our pastor and his family to love people, which is what we are. We can't afford to pay him much, so he or she must depend upon gifts from others. We admit that his presence with us for five or six years will not enhance his Pastor Information Form.

"If our pastor is just out of seminary and is scared stiff to come to our community, which is not even in main stream Alaska, that is fine. It is really a good place to live and we will love him or her. Come to think of it, it should be a him or a her, a handyman type because there are various things around the manse, or parsonage to you Methodist types, that need fixing and we can find all sorts of things to fill his or her free time.

"We can give our pastor some experiences that no other pastor in the denomination will ever experience. We don't even want you to pay people to come to church by giving them candy or presents or sexy movies. That has been tried on us by other religious groups and we resent those who did it. We have had some really wonderful pastors who we loved and still love, though they are no longer with us. We also have some deeply spiritual folks who are lay people but who are super faithful to our congregation. If you are a new young pastor then we can give you some helpful ideas about your ministry. We have had all sorts and some of them really appreciated the training they got here in Olgoonik.

"We will invite you to some meals that you would not believe, eating foods that you never thought that you would eat. We would like you to stay with us for several years. Some people come, talk a lot, take a lot of pictures and then leave on a later plane on the same day. We have been photographed, studied, questioned and almost put in glass cases, but we want a pastor who will stay with us.

"We would suggest that you will be present for some strange ministries. We even had a situation where a grave was accidentally exposed and a group of people came real fast to examine the body, because he had been frozen for hundreds of years so they could study the people of that time. We want to see the lights burning late into the evening in the manse and know that the pastor is there for us. (Sure we know that he is working on his sermon because he was very busy this past week, marrying a couple, burying a couple of folks and working with Maggie and Dennis who are having troubles in their family!) When we are snow-bound we want him to be snow-bound too. That being bound by snow will not stop the worship services and for that matter the singing would warm up the room, regardless of how many degrees below zero it is on the outside.

"Oh, yes, and did we mention that in the summer we have daylight all night long but that in the winter there is no need to worry about sun-burn. 'Sides, we don't have any dermatologists here, or for that matter doctors or dentists either. You have to fly to Barrow, or possibly Fairbanks or Anchorage for those services. Moon-burn may be more of a problem.

"We'd like to thank those churches that had those other advertisements, up above. I don't think that any of those folk who might apply to those churches will want to come to Olgoonik anyway. I hope that they are successful in finding just the pastor that they wish. Some day we would like to visit one or more of their services, but for now we just want someone who will preach God's love to each of us and show that love in the life he lives among us, yes, both pastor and also God.

"That Southern hospitality is really not quite right here in Olgoonik. But we do have a lot of Northern hospitality, to the extent that we take care of everyone in town, often whether they want to be taken care of or not. By the way, ours is a dry town. We do all we can to keep liquor out of the village so that our elders and our kids will be safe. If you use liquor then please do not apply. We still have problems with liquor that is smuggled into town, and if you use it we all will know. I bet those other towns are not dry. This is a small town and it is hard for people to keep secrets from each other, but if you are genuine then we will know it. If you follow Jesus the Christ, we will gladly follow you and him also.

"We are not able to pay for our pastor to bring a lot of junk because everything is flown in unless you wish a long snowmobile ride. So it would be wise if you had some relative in the lower forty-eight who would keep your junk. You really don't need it here, anyway. Think about it, we'd love to have you come to serve God with us."

"Gracious god, you love each of us the way you love each of them down there in the lower forty-eight. Help us to grow in our love of you so that we can share that love with others. We thank you that you send your son to the common people, because that is what we are. In your son's name we pray. Amen."

AND WHOSE TRIP ARE YOU ON?

"In the church in Antioch there were prophets and teachers: Barnabas,
Simeon called Niger, Lucius of Cyrene, Manaen (who had been brought
up with Herod the tetrarch) and Saul. While they were worshiping
the Lord and fasting, the Holy Spirit said, 'Set apart for me Barnabas
and Saul for the work to which I have called them.' So after they had
fasted and prayed, they placed their hands on them and sent them off."
Acts 13:1-3

THE LEADERS OF THE EARLY church were very careful about who they sent to
the various places where churches would be established. The probability of
martyrdom was ever present and the missionaries were devoted to telling the
message of Jesus the Messiah. If enough people responded, then a worshiping
body would be formed and the missionaries would continue on to other
communities. A failure could result in a church never being established or
possibly in their own death.

The leaders of this 2008 church, in the Lower Forty - Eight had wanted
this mission 'thing' to really get off the ground. They had held back some
mission money and decided that their folks needed to visit a mission station
and really find out what it was all about. They heard a lot from those people
in the mission church in the remote part of Alaska, but that was not the same
thing as seeing for themselves. They would also take lots of pictures so that
the people back home who could not travel would get a better idea of what
was happening.

So there were car washes, garage sales, and kids cutting logs and splitting
firewood. The group in the Lower Forty-Eight church got sponsorships from
various folks in the congregation. Next, letters were sent out to people in the
community, and then to relatives until just about every source of funds had
been used.

The church leaders provided money from the budget for the rest of the
expenses so things were set. They were just going to let those who had worked
go, but at the last moment there were other kids, and also a couple of parents
that insisted that they also attend. They had a training session where the

congregation took turns speaking and then the kids would do some singing and if there was a time and place they would put on a skit.

It was intended that the visiting mission group would work in the Arctic community, but no one was too sure just what they would be doing, or what they would need. One of the men thought it wise to include some hammers and even some sixteen penny nails, and they had bought all the food that they would need. They even bought some extra food so that the pastor and his family could eat with them. They would be sleeping in the social hall but would use the "bathroom" in the manse. They didn't quite understand why they couldn't use the one in the social hall until they found out that there wasn't one there.

They were met at the plane and a four-wheeler was used to make several trips for their gear, but they had to walk into town. It was only a short walk anyway, but they felt that it did not seem too welcoming. The pastor explained the shyness of the people, and said that after the week they would be better received. The pastor also was not quite sure what the visitors would be doing. There seemed to be no carpenters in the group, so some of the repairs to the social hall would have to wait. There was some scrap lumber in the corner of the village and the elders of the village said that they could use it. The kids wanted to carry it with the four wheeler, but the pastor wisely kept the keys in his pocket.

The pastor's wife felt inundated. Her stove was the only cooking source so the women who were the cooks came in and took over. They wisely invited the pastor and his family to eat with them. Then came the problem of the bathroom, or the one hole-er, or the chemical toilet. With so many using it, it filled up fast and the pastor took the 55 gallon drum to the storage area. From there it would be taken and dumped during the winter and returned with another empty barrel. It seemed that the first and last thing he did each day was to take the 55 gallon drum to the storage area and continue to empty the chemical toilet.

Meanwhile the scrap lumber was brought and using some base boards they built a walkway to the front of the church. There were not enough hammers for everyone, but they had enough blisters so they took turns. Then the kids decided to play games with the village kids who arrived to watch the visitors. The games were fun and there was a good fellowship between the visitors and the local kids. On Sunday the worship service was really good. The visitors took over the service and the pastor did not have to preach. Instead he sat with his wife and children. In spite of the chemical toilet duties he was warming up to the people who had come to help.

It was soon time for the visitors to leave and the sidewalk was finished. The pastor sighed a sigh of relief that he was almost finished carrying 55 gallon drums to the storage area and finally the plane came. The visitors decided to carry their own baggage to the plane and with tears the kids hugged all around and said goodbye. The pastor was there with his wife. They had gotten to know the folks and there was a good fellowship. The plane had delivered the mail, so the pastor carried the mail bag back to town and waited for the postmaster to sort the mail.

The last letter to be sorted was a letter from the executive of the mission board. As he walked home with a truly tired step he read, "Due to a decrease in giving we have determined to close your mission station. We appreciate the long and regular service that you have rendered, but financially we are unable to provide support. We will assist you in finding another parish. Regards in Him."

"Gracious God, you have given us opportunities to be of service. We appreciate those opportunities, but help us to understand that sometimes our eagerness to know is more of a disturbance than an assist to your ultimate mission.

Help us to prayerfully determine where we can be of service, where we need to go or possibly where we need to stay away from so that your will truly is active. This we pray in the name of Jesus the Christ. Amen."

LIVING TRANSPARENTLY

"Greet all the saints in Christ Jesus. The brothers who are
with me send greetings. All the saints send you greetings,
especially those who belong to Caesar's household. The grace
of the Lord Jesus Christ be with your spirit. Amen."
Philippians 4:21-23

ONE OF THE THINGS WE face as we live in a small Arctic village is the fact of transparency. This means that everything that you do and say is exposed to everyone else. The main means of communication is the CB (citizens band) radio and almost everyone has one in their home. It is kept on all the time. At the other end of the room there usually is a regular long wave radio which broadcasts from Barrow or possibly Kotzebue. The long wave radio is likewise kept on just about all the time.

There is also the mukluk telegraph, the ability to know what is going on in your own village and also other villages with people whom you know.

That means that you are always involved in everything that goes on all the time. You know who arrived in the village on the plane today and every day that you spend in the village. You all know who is leaving the village, and who is sick. To borrow a phrase from another culture, "Don't talk stink about anyone because everyone will know that you did."

The children of the village are raised by the entire village, and if you and your wife or husband are having troubles it is the problem of the entire village. They all know the problem and who to blame. Whether or not they know the entire story is another question, but you better believe that they all have their opinions and may give them at the drop of a hat.

If you or someone in your family gets drunk, then the entire village knows where to point the finger because the village is dry and there are folks who fervently believe that everyone should abide by that village decision. It almost takes the fun out of trying to keep liquor. Likewise, if you are once caught with liquor, then for the next ten or so years you will be suspect, and every time liquor is mentioned your face will appear before everyone's eyes.

When you were young and you fell in love, your lover probably came from the same village. That means that if you marry you are joining two village families together. If your lover came from some other village, then every time that the village is mentioned the person makes sure that you know the news, and the mukluk communication continues.

The main Alaska Native Service Hospital is in Anchorage, a new facility that is a wonderful health facility. All the Alaskan native villagers who need medical attention are given treatment there until they return to their home communities. That means that everyone living in Anchorage who knows that individual, or knows of the village of that person comes to visit. Therefore the hospital is a continual social gathering place for villagers.

Entering the hospital you can see the Savoonga folks in that corner, the Gambell folks over there, the Olgoonik people by the front door, the Nuiqsut people in that corner, and the Barrow folks there in the middle of the room. It goes on and on. They are catching up on the news, at least the person's interpretation of the news and it also means that some native foods are brought and shared with other folks from the home village. Occasionally a stranger from another village will 'drift' into a group to share in the muktuk, which he has missed for the last several years.

Transparent living also has its advantages. If everyone knows of a problem then everyone is concerned. If needed, the children of the family will be taken care of. If the family is low on food, there are many others who will help in feeding the family. Truly the children are raised by the village, and in each village there is an abundance of warm-hearted pride in the way that they take care of their own.

As we move in and through the Christian church we find that transparent living is a fact of fellowship and concern. Individuals have come together from all over the community and they become special persons who represent their corner of the community. They are united by a common relationship, a common love that is understood by all in attendance. The more activities that are participated in the more they feel a part of the fellowship, until the time comes to the children when the word church means those who gather every Sunday to worship and fellowship together.

Those in the community who have no time for worship or church activities do not understand and can not realize how close is the fellowship that church people have. So it is also true that as the members of the congregation move to other communities, they seek the fellowship that they appreciated in their last place of residence. Soon they are more involved in the community than those who have lived secularly all of their lives in that place.

At the beginning and the ending of many of Paul's letters to the various Christian Churches, he expresses the fellowship that he feels. An interesting study is to follow the names and try to determine what each of the persons did in the early churches.

The prefix 'trans' means 'across', 'through' or to 'convey from place to place.' So the word transparent really does convey what happens in a village. All the pride and concern of the entire group and the individuals who make it up is felt by all the citizens of the community, and each becomes a parent to everyone else, whether the other person is younger or is older. Likewise, in the Christian faith there is a tie that binds us all together, regardless of culture, nationality, or age, sexual preference or denominational beliefs. We are truly one people, who have one father God and one lord, Jesus the Christ.

"Father God, help us to live our faith, not forcing our will on others but willingly showing the force of your will in all of our lives. Help us to make practical our love that it might serve your purpose that all folks on the planet might realize your love to and for them, shown in the death and resurrection of your son, Jesus the Christ, in whose name we pray. Amen."

I THINK THAT I SHALL
NEVER SEE - A TREE

"Blessed is the man who does not walk in the counsel of the wicked, or stand in the way of sinners or sit in the seat of mockers. But his delight is in the law of the Lord, and on his law he meditates day and night. He is like a tree planted by streams of water, which yields its fruit in season and whose leaf does not wither. Whatever he does prospers."
Psalm 1:1-3

THE YOUNG PEOPLE PILED OUT of the bus and almost immediately sat on the church's front steps and stared at the trees. If you spoke to them they answered, but they kept staring at the trees that were surrounding the church, tall Sitka Spruce and Hemlock some fifty and sixty feet high.

One boy walked over and touched a tree, as though it were going to bite, then he stepped back and laughed, "Hey, guys, I touched a tree. It has rough bark just like the books say."

These youngsters had left their Eskimo village early that morning, flown to Kotzebue and then flown again to Anchorage. There they boarded a larger plane and were now in Juneau. They had been driven over in a bus and were now waiting for supper supplied by our congregation.

Behind all this was a dream of Dr. Paul Jensen, of the University of Oregon, who wanted to show the village children what the lower forty-eight was really like. His was really a dangerous venture for if anything happened to the kids the entire future of the village would be threatened. He had taken the entire village youth population and was in charge of them for two weeks.

This was the first day and the children had never seen a tree. A few may have noticed the small trees they flew over as they took off from Anchorage. They were very small trees that had never had a chance to grow as they were in a wasteland swamp.

The village from which they came had no trees and most of the children had never left the village or the hunting camps located along the shore of the Arctic Ocean.

They had never seen the "forest" at Nome. Actually, the Nome forest was composed of all the worn out Christmas trees, taken out and planted on the ice, but from town it looked like a miniature forest. Of course when the ice melted the forest disappeared. These children had never been in Nome however, and therefore they had never seen a real tree.

We are not too sure that the youth ever realized that we talked with them for they spent all their time looking at the trees, even taking their plates outside so they could spend more time with the trees.

They had a special experience when two or three eagles came and perched on the very top of the trees in front of the church. These trees had taken all the nutrients out of the soil and were beginning to die, starting at the top. "Shree," the eagle seemed to say, "I'm way up here and can see a great distance and I am doing something that you can't do." One of the boys thought that he could climb the tree, but the trunk was too large and there were no limbs within fifteen feet of the ground.

The reason for the lack of trees on the Arctic Slope is that the roots of trees have to go somewhere and when all the ground is permanently frozen (permafrost) the trees do not have a chance to grow. This was just the first day of two weeks when the youth would grow to appreciate the rest of the country of which they were a part.

So it is with the rest of us who live in the lower forty-eight, which to many Inupiat children means beginning at the southern edge of their town. We need to place ourselves in a position to learn not the intricacies of modern life but rather the truths and traditions of the former, but sometimes present members of our society. Eskimo values which they take for granted are values that we need to examine. A self-sufficient but neighbor-dependent lifestyle is something that we need to duplicate in the population locations in the lower forty-eight. Interest in all our neighbors, regardless of their age or social status or cultural traits should be sharpened.

Today is June 14th, known as flag day. It is a day when we put out our flags because that is the patriotic thing to do. But patriotic is a word that means a relationship with our forefathers. They brought to this nation a sense of freedom, where justice and righteousness were values that they held to be truths. Our freedom is based on the value of each person God has put on the planet earth, and we hold these truths to be valuable that all men are born equal. The bases for our beliefs are found in God's word, that resulting in a culture that has Christian love for its foundation.

That leads to the fatherhood of God, the creator of all of us, whether thousands of years ago or this morning in the maternity section of the local hospital. We are God's children and brothers and sisters to all who surround us.

I think that I shall never see a tree, but that I think of the children who saw real trees for the first time in their lives. May they continue to learn the deep values of our culture as we strive to realize the deep values that they hold dear.

"Gracious God, you created us and still sustain us. You have surrounded us with loving families and friends and in their love we see your hand of creation. Be with us as we continue to live our lives, thankful for all we have received and also jealous that we might share it with those who do not have as much as we. In your son's name we pray. Amen."

MOSQUITOS

"Listen, my son, to your father's instructions and do not forsake your
mother's teaching. They will be a garland to grace your head and
a chain to adorn your neck. My son, if sinners entice you, do not
give in to them. If they say, 'Come along with us; let's lie in wait for
someone's blood, let's waylay some harmless soul; let's swallow them
alive, like the grave, and whole, like those who go down to the pit;'"
Proverbs 1:8-12

THE BOOK OF PROVERBS WAS very important to the Hebrew faith. A knowledge
of the entire book was necessary for a young Hebrew boy to pass his Son of
the Covenant examination. There are various sections, not always chapter
designations and I'd suggest you read the entire Exhortation to Embrace
Wisdom section, Proverbs 1:8-19.

It was our first day on the Alcan and we were traveling during the early
spring through the Yukon. We must have been the first travelers in the
campground, for there was a host waiting for us. The host were mosquitos.
Before I dashed to the shower I counted 155 on the screened window of the
car, and it was totally impossible to be accurate in my counting as more and
more were coming.

The Arctic villages also have a problem with mosquitos, and I, a lonely
tunik, have the solution. We live on the edge of a marsh and those who warned
us about living here, a flood plain and also so close to mosquito heaven, did
not really study the problem. There is a solution to the mosquito problem.

First let's define the problem. On the second of July the mosquitos arrive
in each one of the Arctic villages. The reason for this is that the entire Arctic
slope is a marsh, or swamp or wetlands. You can choose the designated
title. However the slope is perma-frosted, and that means that the surface
ground does not thaw until about the middle of June. The tundra then
contains millions of small lakes, each replete with its own mass of larva of
mosquitos.

It takes the larva about two or three weeks to hatch out, and all the female
mosquitos immediately look for a source of blood upon which they feed in
order to feed their new young mosquitos. Knowing this, let's admit that the

best antidote for mosquitos are swallows. The problem is that the swallows could not take the entire spring and summer flying to the north slope villages because as soon as they'd arrive they would have to turn around and head back south before it got cold.

Enter Alaska Airlines. Alaska Airlines is not only a passenger carrier it is also a freight carrier. They make money by not spending time loading aircraft, but rather by flying so they have large cargo containers called Igloos, that just fit inside the Boeing 737 aircraft. These are loaded into the planes with a front end loader, which takes only a few minutes, and the plane again takes off.

Because they are community conscious with respect to public relations Alaska could fly empty igloos to the airport nearest to San Juan Capistrano. There they will turn the igloos over to the local residents who are experts in the raising of swallows. Each igloo would have a name such as Olgoonik, Point Lay, Barrow, Kaktovik, Nuiksut, Aquasuk, and possibly Anaktuvik Pass and Delta Junction. The name is the final summer destination of the igloo. Each igloo proves a nesting area for several swallow families.

We know that the swallows are the best antidote for mosquitos, and also that they have extreme homing abilities. They fly from San Juan Capistrano throughout the west and arrive back in town at a designated time.

On the 1st of July the swallows will be provided with two days worth of feed and then placed in the igloos and Alaska Airlines will fly the igloos to Barrow for immediate distribution to the designated villages.

On the 2nd of July the igloos will arrive in their designated villages be opened and the swallows released. Inside a month the mosquitos will be gone and the swallows now will be waddling from overeating (should we call it the big gulp) The swallows will then be flown back to San Juan Capistrano and arrive before all their aunts, uncles and cousins do (and they can tell their relatives about their trip to Alaska how they saw polar bears, and all the other arctic animals, even if they didn't) and the problem has been solved.

After a couple of years of this activity the swallows can be retired and Alaska Airlines can return to flying fish and other freight. The villagers can do something other than swear at the mosquitos that are no longer there.

A few problems would have to be worked out, but this tunic sees no harm in trying anyway. The good thing about this solution is that everyone is the hero, the villages, the swallow trainers, Alaska Airlines and, well, I will wish to remain anonymous.

It seems that our world is filled with irritants. Possibly they are no-see-ems that are found in the warm wonderful, thick, lush, grass of the Southern part of the Lower 48, or possibly it is the poison oak or poison ivy that infests many of the Californian hills and also trails, or the Haole koa that magically materializes everywhere in Hawai'i. Perhaps they are dandelions that automatically materialize when you think that they have been eradicated, or even wasps when you really wanted honey bees, to say nothing of the blackberry bushes that exude more thorns than they do berries.

Irritants are everywhere. I wonder if I am an irritant to anyone, that I try to go places that I do not belong, to do things that irritate others and yet of which I am unaware.

"Gracious God, humor us as we try to solve the irritants that we face daily. We extend our love to you as you have extended your love to us. Help us to see the wonderful joy of living in the great land that you have provided for us. This we pray in the name of Jesus, the Christ. Amen."

THE LONGEST DAY OF THE YEAR

"Shadrach, Meshach and Abednego replied to the king, 'O Nebuchadnezzar, we do not need to defend ourselves before you in this matter. If we are thrown into the blazing furnace, the God we serve is able to save us from it, and he will rescue us from your hand, O king. But even if he does not, we want you to know, O king, that we will not serve your gods or worship the image of gold you have set up.' "
Daniel 3:16-18

THERE ARE TWO DAYS, PARTICULARLY in the life of the Alaskan, that stand out almost before all others. One of them is the 21st of December, admittedly lost in the Christmas rush, and it is the shortest day of the year. It is a day of hope before we know that the days are beginning to get longer, that spring is on the way and that summer will soon follow, though sometimes it is delayed.

The other day is the 21st of June and that is because it is the longest day of the year and there is no better place to celebrate it than on the northern coast of the State of Alaska. It was the 21st day of June and the grandfather and granddaughter were standing looking north at midnight. There the sun, that solar orb that is so often missing in Alaska, stared them in their face, about 15 degrees above the horizon. As the grandfather said, "That is due north."

In some places the longest day of the year is celebrated by a baseball game, played at midnight without lights, that is held just to emphasize that it is the longest day of the year. In other places it is a discouraging thing because the fourth of July that follows in just a few days is always the occasion for shooting off fireworks. They are very unimpressive, however, when the sun is still shining. It is discouraging to spend thousands of dollars on fireworks and then have the sun shine on all your activities. What's more the fireworks are not just the large commercial fireworks but also the home Roman candles and rockets that are shot from the street in front of your house, and that litter the streets for days until the next heavy rain washes the blasted paper and cardboard down the drain.

The longest day of the year can be something other than the 21st of June. It may be a wedding day, and the days seems to go on for ever. It begins with a period of dating and then finally selecting the individual with whom you want to spend the rest of your life. There is an announcement as you gain a diamond ring and then set a date. If grandmother's or mother's wedding dress is an option, then alterations must be made until it is just a perfect fit. If those dresses are not available, then a trip, (or trips) to a store will determine what you shall wear, along with bridesmaids.

In some Hawaiian weddings there will be also a determination of what sashes you or the groomsmen will wear. There will be counseling, hopefully five sessions exploring all the various situations that you will encounter, so that you can meet them together as a loving team rather than as competitors. You are not looking just for a sparkling wedding but for a long-term love-filled marriage resulting in a wonderful family.

Then there is a longest day of the year when your first, or any child, is born. There is a nine month period when morning sickness is a problem, followed by a swelling as your pregnancy endures, or so it seems. Finally the time for delivery is present and there is the strain of hoping that the baby to be born will have ten fingers, (well, eight fingers and two thumbs) and also have all the rest of the parts of a unique body, a melding of two personalities. All your friends will tell you that he has your mother's nose, father's chin and on and on it goes.

Then there is the longest day of the year when you lose a loved one, whether known beforehand because of a lingering illness, or tragic loss of life through accident or undetermined physical ailment. "It does not seem possible that he or she was with us just a few hours ago and now is gone forever." The Christian witness would state something different, but for those without any hope for eternity such a loss can be life-changing for the future. So the longest days of the year come and go. Of course the days really do not change. They are still twenty four hours of sixty minutes each and a minute still contains 60 seconds.

The scripture passage at the beginning of this parable, tells of three men who were determined to serve their God, and not the god of Nebuchadnezzar. They remind me of all the "ifs" that come to humans in a lifelong quest to serve God. It leads my thinking of the poem "If" by Rudyard Kipling that was early learned in my youth.

If you can keep your head when all about you
Are losing theirs and blaming it on you;
If you can trust yourself when all men doubt you,
But make allowance for their doubting too;
If you can wait and not be tired by waiting,
Or, being lied about, don't deal in lies,
Or, being hated, don't give way to hating,
And yet don't look too good, nor talk too wise;

If you can dream - and not make dreams your master;
If you can think - and not make thoughts your aim;
If you can meet with triumph and disaster
And treat those two impostors just the same;
If you can bear to hear the truth you've spoken
Twisted by knaves to make a trap for fools,
Or watch the things you gave your life to broken,
And stoop and build them up with worn out tools.

If you can make one heap of all your winnings
And risk it on one turn of pitch-and-toss,
And lose, and start again at your beginnings
And never breathe a word about your loss;
If you can force your heart and nerve and sinew
To serve your turn long after they are gone,
And so hold on when there is nothing in you
Except the Will which says to them: "Hold on";

If you can talk with crowds and keep your virtue ,
Or walk with kings - nor lose the common touch;
If neither foes nor loving friends can hurt you;
If all men count with you, but none too much;
If you can fill the unforgiving minute
With sixty second's worth of distance run-
Yours is the Earth and everything that's in it,
And - which is more - you'll be a Man, my son!

"Gracious God, we have determined to serve you whether the days be long or short. We have determined that to the best of our ability we will perform that service with each waking moment, not determined by our own desires but rather by our dependence on you and your love. Help us to understand the life, death and resurrection of your son, Jesus whom if we have seen, then we have seen you, for we pray in his name. Amen."

THE IGLOO

"Do not let your hearts be troubled, Trust in God; trust also
in me. In my Father's house are many rooms; if it were not
so, I would have told you. I am going there to prepare a place
for you. And if I go and prepare a place for you, I will come
back and take you to be with me that you also may be where
I am. You know the way to the place where I am going."
John 14:1-4

WHENEVER THE WORD ESKIMO IS spoken, the listener usually conjures up
a picture of a snow house, the Igloo. Millions still believe that all Eskimos
live in igloos and to convince them otherwise is an endless task. An igloo is
a temporary snow house, built usually at the beginning of a storm when the
hunter needs to rest during the howling wind and blowing snow.

At Sheldon Jackson School, in a gathering of young people from both
Southeastern and Interior Alaska, there was a discussion concerning the
Eskimo folks. It was discovered that none of the Eskimo students, Yupic or
Inupiat, had ever seen an igloo. Therefore, the senior boys dorm supervisor,
whose home was in Chicago, built an igloo. The snow was just right, the
blocks were strong, and before long there was an igloo out in front of his
dorm.

Many years ago I also attempted to build an igloo. We lived in Hamburg,
New York, just a few miles from Buffalo at the Eastern end of Lake Erie. That
area is known for its heavy snow, so much so that where other towns have fire
engines in their parades, in Hamburg they parade with snow plows. So in my
Junior High wisdom I thought that I could build one.

There were no problems stacking the blocks of snow up the side walls
but every time that I began to enclose the walls the blocks came tumbling
down. "The snow was too powdery," was my excuse, and it remained until
the weather had warmed. Then I didn't need snow, I needed an umbrella. My
mother was not going to allow me to sleep in it anyway, so I ceased to pretend
to be an Eskimo.

The official igloo is used when folks are hunting and don't want to rush
back to the village. The snow usually is packed, so the blocks are easy to cut

and stack. There is an entrance through which you crawl, and the inside is always much warmer than the exterior with the wind blowing. When the storm passes, you leave the igloo and it ceases to exist when the weather warms up.

To an extent, we all live in igloos, a temporary dwelling, even those who have lived in their homes for a long period of time. The homes that we build are temporary, particularly in this day and age when folks move so much. I can remember homes on Pleasant Avenue (site of the igloo-less structure) and also Long Avenue in Hamburg, and on Woodwell and Dalzell place in Pittsburgh. I lived in many places as I moved extensively in the Army, and then lived in Sterling, Kansas. I have lived in Sitka, Klawock, Auke Bay and Eagle River in Alaska; Waimea (in the island governor's home) on Kaua'i, in Surprise, Arizona, and now in Ferndale, Washington. Each home was temporary.

But let's go a step further, each of us lives in a house, not eternal which we shall leave some day. The funeral service then talks about a heavenly home that shall be with God in the heavens.

My home has changed much. I was a small child and then began to grow tall. As time went on, my 'house' developed the need for glasses and then began to become more robust (that is preferable to getting fat), until the house developed wrinkles and had an improvement in the auditory system. The house has lost much of its strength at the present time. Fortunately I have been able to control the robustness, but the time will come when I vacate this temporary house (temporary when considered in light of an eternity with God) and I will leave my last igloo.

I have a responsibility even now to take care of my igloo. I exercise and walk to make sure that all the parts keep moving. I have had some minor changes made through surgery and, of course, I just sorted the pills that I take so that I take the right number of the right pills to keep all my systems working in proper order.

I have a building inspector who checks my pump to keep the blood circulating and some of my plumbing needs some alterations, but so far not to the point of calling in a plumber.

I have avoided those things that would abuse my igloo, and have been fortunate in that the carpenters who worked me over were concerned about my staying alive and continuing them on my list of payees.

I thank God for the igloo that I inhabit, for all the things that he has provided to keep it in as good working order as possible. His word contains many wonderful and helpful comments about how I maintain my igloo and I gladly recommend the suggestions found in the physical and spiritual manual governing my igloo-the Bible

Though I would prefer to keep going in my igloo, as I am always curious about what is going to happen tomorrow, or what happened today that is only reported tomorrow, I presume that when the master builder is ready to take over my igloo, I will be willing to part with it. It is really his, anyway, so he is just getting what he owns. It is my responsibility to keep it in good working order as long as I can, and that is what I do.

"Loving God, I thank you for the igloos that I, my family and friends inhabit. We acknowledge that they are temporary, and the final home will be with you. As we did not know about the homes we inhabited before we lived in them, so we do not know about all the features of the heavenly home that we will inhabit, and we will move on in faith. Increase our faith for we look forward to a new appreciation of your love. This we pray in the name of your son, Jesus the Christ. Amen."

FATHER'S DAY IN OLGOONIK

"This then is how you should pray: 'Our Father in heaven, hallowed
be your name, your kingdom come, your will be done on earth as it
is in heaven. Give us today our daily bread. Forgive us our debts, as
we also have forgiven our debtors. And lead us not into temptation
but deliver us from the evil one.' For if you forgive men when they sin
against you, your heavenly Father will also forgive you. For if you do
not forgive men their sins, your Father will not forgive your sins."
Matthew 6:9-15

IT IS FATHERS DAY IN Olgoonik and we hear on the news that a man has killed
his wife and buried her along with their two children, who were still alive. And
another man has thrown his children off a bridge and hundreds or thousands
more have abandoned their families throughout the country. So many have
given up their responsibility for their families that one of the political leaders
of the country has said, "We need fathers to realize that responsibility does
not end at conception. We need them to realize that what makes you a man
is not the ability to have a child, it's the courage to raise one."

Here in Olgoonik we think of the fathers who have passed down their
love for their family, have given their knowledge of a way of life to their
children and who have vowed to stay with their families for as long as they
live. Father and son can work together whether it is hunting or whaling, or
hauling water.

The hymn for today is;

"Faith of our Fathers, living still in spite of dungeon fire and sword
O how our hearts beat high with joy whenever we hear that glorious word
Faith of our fathers! God's great power shall win all nations unto thee
And through the truth that comes from God mankind shall then be truly
  free
Faith of our fathers! we will love both friend and foe in all our strife
And preach thee too, as love knows how by kindly words and virtuous life
Faith of our fathers, holy faith! We will be true to thee till death."

So in Olgoonik today we think of the fathers of this congregation, men and also women, who have been active in the growth of this congregation.

There was Dr. Henry W. Griest who lived in Barrow but along with elder Roy Ahmaogak organized the church June 24, 1923, before many of us were born. Dr. Newhall also took Dr. Griest's place and Rev. Roy Ahmaogak was active in translating the scriptures into our language.

Rev.Klerekoper also served the church, coming every three months to be in the church and Percy Ipalook took charge when there were no ordained pastors. Rev.Frank (Lou) Grafton served until his retirement and Rev. Samuel Simmonds was pastor until his retirement.

Patricia Berg came as a stated supply and the Rev. Roger Kemp served as our latest full time pastor.

Each of the loyal 'fathers' along with the laymen and women of the church brought an emphasis that was true to their personalities but at the same time totally dependent upon the scriptures. They were individuals who spent much time in the building of the congregation and in service to the community.

Many of them have gone now to be with our heavenly father and it is to his love that each individual pointed. God is referred to but is given many different titles, twenty one that can be identified in the Old Testament. They are terms that show a part of who he is and we call them revelations as he reveals who he is. Some of these are strong one, the self-existent one, righteousness, sanctify-er, provider, the I Am, and just about every other strong everlasting and almighty name is used.

It was when Jesus Christ was given to the world that God was referred to as "Our Father." Not only is the relationship established that he is the father of all, but that he is ours. We do not own him, he owns us. Each of the forefathers-of-our-congregation tried to show that tight relationship between God and us.

When we pray the Lord's Prayer we realize that although we are about the furthest Northwest congregation in our country, we still are united with all other Christian folks; not only in our country but throughout the world. We may differ when it comes to the "sins," "debts" or "trespasses," but we are united by the phrase, "Our Father."

"Father God, we seek to honestly be your children, to live with the love that you have given us through Jesus the Christ. Help us to translate that love into the deeds and thoughts that guide our daily living and we in turn will pass that love on to our children. Gracious Father, may every day we live be your day. We seek your will. In Jesus's name we pray. Amen."

ROTTEN ICE THEOLOGY

"As I urged you when I went into Macedonia, stay there in
Ephesus so that you may command certain men not to teach
false doctrines any longer nor to devote themselves to myths and
endless genealogies. These promote controversies rather than God's
work - which is by faith. The goal of this command is love, which
comes from a pure heart and a good conscience and a sincere faith.
Some have wandered away from these and turned to meaningless
talk. They want to be teachers of the law, but they do not know
what they are talking about or what they so confidently affirm.
I Timothy 1:3-7

THERE ARE SOME THINGS IN the Arctic that those of us who have been born
here take for granted, but which are seldom understood by the taniks that
visit us. Let me explain.

We live in the Arctic and take our way of life for granted, though we are
always trying to improve ourselves. We used to paddle our whale boats but we
now use engines, sometimes at the aft of the craft but more often the engine
is located in the center of the whale boat, and that way it is not in the way if
we are squeezed together by an ice flow or are busy harpooning a whale.

When a whale is sighted the captain of the boat calls the crew, and we
slide the boat over the surface of the ice to where we can launch the boat. One
man handles the motor and steers while others prepare for the battle that will
come with the whale.

Another man makes sure the harpoon line is clear, and that a tangle will
not drag a man into the ocean. If there are two or more boats after the same
whale, then the senior whaling captain will be in charge and we all do what
he says. It is good to be responsible for harpooning the whale, but it is more
important to get the whale. The entire village will get meat regardless of who
harpoons the whale, but of course there is lots of pride in having a good boat
that brings in a lot of whales.

When the whale is harpooned, at least once and sometimes two or three
times, a towing rope is fastened to the front of the whaling boat and the whale
swims along dragging us along with him. A man is in charge of the rope and if

the whale decides to sound, or go down to the bottom of the ocean, the rope man has to give him slack or the whale will drag us all to the bottom. It has happened. When the whale becomes tired or dies, we attach the rope to the back of the boat and drag the whale to the edge of the ice or to shore. Then we have the battle of dragging the whale to a place where we will cut up the meat and distribute it to the various families of the village.

If the ice is rotten, or thin and just a skim of ice, then it is almost impossible to drag the whale to shore, or even to get the whale boat to the launching water.

Rotten ice looks like solid ice to the cheechako, but we know the difference. Sometimes young kids, who do more doing than thinking, will ride their snow machines on the rotten ice and they are rewarded by the machine breaking through the ice. Then they lose a five thousand dollar machine. Once a snow machine has sunk into salt water it is no good for anything, but some kids just don't learn.

Rotten ice reminds us of some kinds of theology that are not solid, and cannot be trusted. It looks good but it can't be trusted. This can be found occasionally in the Bible in the Old Testament (covenant) and the New Testament (Covenant). This kind of theology crept into the church in the New Testament times and still is very prevalent in today's churches. There are many who preach with wonderful sound systems, lots of entertaining interludes and who have gregarious personalities, but they and their theology are 'thin ice.'

Jesus Christ came to earth to help us know what God wants of us. God first instituted a system of sacrifice and then of keeping the laws, but the laws were to help us to know the right way, and to guide people who were wandering into the way of God. (Jesus said, " I am the WAY, and the TRUTH and the LIFE"). Many people interpreted the laws in such a way that a legal person could get around just about any law that God had given. Jesus came to make sure that our theology was solid, that it had a solid meaning of God showing love to us and us showing love to each other and to him. Some people could not understand that and still wanted to live by having laws that they could break or alter. It also meant that some folks wanted to spend all their time talking about the laws and to make them so complicated that the common person could not keep track of them.

And there are still some folks today who live by legal standards. One of the lawful things that they have in the lower forty-eight are casinos. These are places where you can hopefully give a little and gain a lot of money. In the middle of casino is "Sin" and in the middle of sin there is "I". Whenever we put ourselves into the middle of anything, or anyone, that can be sin. Then we are skating on 'thin ice'. Our lives, not just our words and fingers, must point to God who showed his extreme love by providing his son to be our savior.

Therefore our theology (theo - God, logos-word) must be that God loves us with a love that is hard for many to understand. This is more important than all laws, though some laws can guide us to it.

Jesus would have us test all our actions against the love expressed, rather than whether it is lawful or not. People could not understand him two thousand years ago and even today people have a hard time understanding. We have the same trouble making people understand that the ice is not solid and that to depend upon thin is to take a very cold salt water bath, without soap.

The solid ice is the hard cold fact that faith in Jesus Christ is the only basis for salvation and a continuing relationship with God. If there are other ways, then God's will be done. We respond to God's word and that is what it said and says.

"Gracious God keep us from legalizing ourselves into corners when your love is the only way for us to go. Help us to understand all our actions so that they will truly show that we are trying to do your will. Give us words to say and lives to live as we face the faithless of the world, so that others might come into our fellowship, for we pray in the name of Jesus the Christ, our savior. Amen."

SEALSKIN WALLETS

"Then the eleven disciples went to Galilee, to the mountain
where Jesus had told them to go. When they saw him, they
worshiped him; but some doubted. Then Jesus came to them and
said, 'All authority in heaven and on earth has been given to me.
Therefore go and make disciples of all nations, baptizing them
in the name of the Father and of the Son and of the Holy Spirit,
and teaching them to obey everything I have commanded you.
And surely I am with you always, to the very end of the age.'"
Matthew 28:16-20

ONE OF THE THINGS THAT you learn in the Arctic is that you must use
everything that you have. If you are a hunter, not only the meat but the
skins, bones and antlers, or tusks must be returned to camp and ultimately
be used.

So it was that the seal was taken, the meat used, the bones used often as
ribs for boats and the skin was also used. One of the women then asked the
question, "What will be do with these scraps that we have left over?" Sitting
in the circle there was much discussion and the question was raised, "Have
we come to the time when we have used everything that we can and the rest
is to be put out?"

Then someone suggested, "Let's make wallets. The leather will be strong
on the inside and the seal skin will be something that the tunic visitors
will cherish. So copying a wallet that one of the women had for the right
dimensions (no sense making something that would not fit in a man's pocket,
though they seldom kept wallets with them) they fashioned a wallet pattern
and produced another item for the tunic tourists.

They delivered and sold many, and it was only later that one of the tour
dealers came to them with a complaint. Because all the skin or fur on the
outside of the wallet went in the same direction they found that the wallets
"crept" up the pockets and fell out on the floors. The fur or hair would catch
on the sides of the pocket and drag the rest of the wallet along with it. Every
time a person walked, the wallet would slowly edge up the person's pocket
with the resulting loss of the wallet if it was not found in time.

The women worked and worked on the project. If the fur was on the inside that defeated the beauty of the wallet and they could not compare with the professionally made, wallets. The result was to stop making the wallets altogether or else to warn the people to expect it.

Actually, most people in the lower forty-eight, beginning in Fairbanks and also Anchorage, spend most of their alert moments in the modern mall. Cities brag about the large malls that they have and malls have defeated the Mom & Pop stores. So people wander from store to store, wondering what they can buy and there is more wallet-ing than there is walking. Of course, now the wallets do not contain money but plastic cards. All three village stores graciously accept your credit cards.

The nation in the lower forty eight has turned into a massive market. There is more interest in a large mall than there is in warm and comfortable homes. There are crammed garages, attics that sag with the weight of stuff and garages that bulge so much with the accumulation that all cars are kept outside. Not only that, many of those bulging garages are larger than the homes here in Olgoonik.

In addition, large storage areas are available where you can rent a garage-sized storage area to keep the things that you want but have no daily need for. There used to be a radio show where Fibber McGee had a closet that was crammed full of things and when the door opened it sounded as though the junk from a thousand homes was falling on the floor. That now describes how many American families now live.

Arctic homes are small compared with those of the lower forty-eight, and in many homes something must go if you plan to bring in something new. If you are going to buy something new then on Saturday there will be a garage sale, or a yard sale to get rid of the excess so you have room for the new thing.

Maybe there is a hidden truth here. Hundreds of tons of stuff come to our country from China, India, Malaysia and other foreign places. Hundreds of thousands of drums of oil come to our country from countless other countries. Maybe what we have to offer the rest of the world is the very simple faith that is found in our arctic villages, a faith that is sufficient and really more important than all the junk and stuff that comes into our country from other places.

Perhaps our faith in Jesus Christ needs to be exported, the simple faith that keeps us going, lovingly, from week to week. One person jokingly remarked that they were the center of the entire earth. From there they could go just about anywhere on the globe. But it is not just a joke. The Sunday evening radio hymn singing can be heard by many throughout the world and through electronic means. By personally going to some of those places we can carry a message of hope and love, and concern and peace between all the people that God has planted on the planet earth - and if there are persons in other places then we have the opportunity, as well as the responsibility to welcome them into the family of God.

There are people in China, India, Iran, Iraq and Russia and in just about every corner of the world-who also hold Jesus Christ to be the son of God, who are brothers and sisters to each one of us here in the Arctic. They may not recognize you, and they probably will not recognize the food that you eat, but they will recognize your faith as being similar to theirs. Through all of us God's will can spread over the earth, all because we made wallets of seal skin.

This is not a new process. There are many here in Alaska, possibly some of your close relatives, who are related to those who are in Siberia. It is natural for you to express your faith which is the most important thing that each one of us has. May God bless us as we meditate, ponder and then plan for the promulgation (a big word that means send out) of our faith

"In humility and the words of St. Francis we pray to you, Father God, that we might be instruments of your peace, that where there is hatred we might show love, where there is malice we might show justice. Grant us serenity to accept the things we cannot change, courage to change the things that we can and wisdom to know the difference. In Christ's name we pray. Amen."

HOW DRY I AM

"Then Jesus' mother and brothers arrived. Standing outside,
they sent someone in to call him. A crowd was sitting around
him, and they told him, 'Your mother and brothers are outside
looking for you.' Then he looked at those seated in a circle around
him and said, "Here are my mother and my brothers! Whoever
does God's will is my brother and sister and mother.'"
Mark 3:31-35

MANY OF THE COMMUNITIES IN Alaska are dry, that is bringing or having liquor or any intoxicating beverage in your possession is illegal. It was not always so, and the battle for making Alaska as dry as it is was not easy. The formation of the Alaska Council of Churches was a combination of many of the cooperating churches in Alaska. It was formed to have fellowship, to understand each other's theology and ways of worship, and to make a Christian witness within the state concerning moral stands.

There were many projects that were attributed to the Alaska Council of Churches, and then its later name and constitution change to the Alaska Christian Conference, (A.C.C.).

In Southeastern Alaska there was an effort to make available to ferry travelers of the Marine Highway system the scheduled worship services for all denominations and congregation in the towns that were served by the Highway. This was not just for the Alaska Council of Churches, but also for other non-cooperating congregations. The effort continued until there were not enough persons to assist in stacking the literature racks in the ferry terminals. Membership in the A.C.C. was not only open to denominations but also to individual churches whose denomination had determined not to take part. This became a thorn of contention.

Another project was the Prayer Card put in Alaska Airlines flights where a meal was served. This was begun by the Alaska Christian Conference and was continued by the management of Alaska Airlines.

A mural was painted by Rie Munoz depicting the pioneer missionaries of the various denominations, and also the publication by Tay Thomas of the very comprehensive book "Cry in the Wilderness".

But it was in another area that the Alaska Christian Conference, as the name was to be officially labeled, was involved. The lay folk, as well as the clergy of the villages and churches of the larger cities, made known their concern about the depth of the problem of alcohol on native people, as well as the white folk of Alaska. Along with the Alaska Federation of Natives and the Alaska Native Brotherhood and the Sisterhood pressure, the A.C.C. put pressure on the legislature to keep alcohol out of the villages.

There were many who fought the issue and claimed that they had a right to drink. At the same time, others said that no one was keeping them in the villages and if they wanted to go 'outside' to the lower forty-eight where they could drink no one would really miss them. It was a very warm issue for several years.

One of the unique things of the Alaska Christian Conference was that in their legal voting during the assembly meetings, the lay folk had equal say with the denomination executives. This was an unknown thing to many of the Hierarchal denomination representatives. Though it was true that often the clergy of a particular denomination kept a close eye on their executive, for the most part the lay folk voted as their consciences led them. One clergyman decided to sit in front of his executive and then to vote his conscience. Strangely he was assigned to a remote preaching station in the Western part of the state soon after the meeting.

The Alaska Christian Conference also held two and three day orientation meetings to assist new pastors to get to know the state, the social agencies that were available and other unique relationships that existed in the state. It was a time of fellowship that was appreciated by both the clergy and lay folk, though this possibly held a strain for the denominational representatives.

A close study of the four gospels in the New Testament, studying the life of Jesus the Christ, reveals that during his ministry Jesus was almost silent on spirituality and how to live a holy life. It would seem natural that he would be vocal in the promulgation of spiritual living, but instead he talked of the individual receiving the Holy Spirit when he or she made a confession of faith. Jesus was more concerned with the relationships that we have with each other and our relationship with God the Father.

Though denominations tend to cite Jesus's teachings in order to positively present some of their doctrinal issues, the verbalized theology of Jesus did not spend much time on spiritual growth even though he knew Old Testament scripture as a whole. He was involved in presenting himself as the Messiah. Even that message of Jesus was misunderstood for most of his ministry, only coming to the awareness of the disciples following his death and resurrection.

Jesus was always attentive to the individuals who came to him and time after time he expressed his belief that each person was very important. Even those who intentionally touched him seemed to gain power to heal illnesses and ultimately to speak out boldly of the truths that Jesus had taught them.

Whereas Jesus spent much time in prayer, normally off by himself early in the morning, prayer has become a very important part of the religious expression, more an open prayer than a memorized repetition or rote prayer. Establishing a normal prayer life strengthens the relationship between God and each of us. The most famous prayer, the Lord's Prayer, is an example of how to pray, not necessarily a rote expression, though the prayer does merit long and meditative examination.

The Alaska Christian Conference has been responsible for maintaining a sober life style for the inhabitants of the villages of Alaska, a life style that many larger towns could emulate but has waned in importance as more and more denominations desire not to take part in its activities. Possibly at a later time when more ecumenism means that denominational representatives feel less threatened, it will return to its highly important place in the life of the Alaskan Church of Jesus the Christ.

"Loving Father of us all, forgive us for the divisions that we establish because we do not totally embrace you as our father. We rejoice that there is no 'corner of heaven' where we can enjoy ourselves with our own kind, as all your children are all of your kind. Keep us open to embrace all who love you, here on earth, as it will be in heaven. In Jesus, our elder brother's name we pray. Amen."

NOT YET, SON

"Paul and his companions traveled throughout the region of Phrygia
and Galatia, having been kept by the Holy Spirit from preaching
one word in the province of Asia. When they came to the border of
Mysia, they tried to enter Bithynia, but the Spirit of Jesus would not
allow them to. So they passed by Mysia and went down to Troas.
During the night Paul had a vision of a man of Macedonia standing
and begging him, 'Come over to Macedonia and help us.' After Paul
had seen the vision, we got ready at once to leave for Macedonia,
concluding that God had called us to preach the gospel to them."
Acts. 16:6-10

THE ESKIMO PEOPLE OF NORTHERN Alaska faced an almost impossible time
during the 1890s. White hunters had just about decimated the walrus and seal
populations, and had driven the survivors out of reach of the Eskimo hunters.
Not only was their economy gone, but also their ability to survive.

Dr. Sheldon Jackson had visited Eastern Russia and had seen the reindeer
herds. He realized that importing reindeer to Alaska could save the Eskimos
from extinction. The American government would not sanction the idea, but
Dr. Jackson raised over $2000 and brought sixteen animals to Unalaska. The
experiment did not work, however probably because Unalaska was too warm.
The government still would not fund the idea so he again raised money and
the next year brought 175 animals to Teller, where the experiment began to
succeed.

Congress then appropriated enough funding to bring over 125 more
reindeer and they began to multiply rapidly as more and more were given
to various communities. The Eskimo were hunters and not herders, so they
needed instruction on herding the animals. Therefore Lapps were brought in
to instruct the Eskimo herders and then the reindeer flourished. After a three-
year period of instruction, the herders were able to be on their own. One of
these herders was the father of Samuel Simmonds. Samuel spent much time
in Olgoonik and ultimately spent 16 years as the very successful pastor of
the church there. The church thrived under his care. As several have stated,

"Samuel was the perfect pastor, to the people, to the community and to other pastors of the parish."

One of his hobbies was the carving of ivory, and he was particularly concerned with carving things that he remembered. The most famous of his carvings is the one of an Eskimo father putting his hand on his son's shoulder. The boy, Samuel, wanted to go whaling to experience the anticipation, the excitement and the ultimate success in whaling, but his father said, "Not yet, Son".

At the present time we live in a generation that possibly needs the words of Samuel's father, "Not yet, son." There are so many things that young people want to do, but they do not want to wait until they are really ready. It is possible for instance, to get a (supposedly) college degree without having to attend any schooling, but "Not yet, son" is something to remember.

There are many who want to be ministers of the gospel and are willing to read books at home, but not attend any campus seminars, (which of course is where the name Seminary comes from) and they do not appreciate the words, "Not yet, son."

In Scripture, we find many times that God has said, "Not yet, son." We forget that God has his timing and that is the correct time. Often it means that further preparation is necessary, yet urgency seems to be the core of life with humans. Everything must happen right now, right here and with me. God often determines that it will happen in his time, after his preparation and possibly with someone else.

God usually has many surprises and excitement in the doing of his will, and when he puts off your desires it is always better for the cause of which he is the sponsor.

I have a small ivory carving of "Not yet, Son" and it reminds me that it is God's timing that is important, and also that God possibly has someone else in mind to do the job. That is good.

Looking through the history of the church in Alaska, both in Southeastern and also in the Interior and Arctic slope I find that often, and to his glory, he has used people in his time and to do his will. That is and should be our prayer. It is not necessary to tell God how to fulfil his will, only to be ready if he calls you.

In our Scripture, Paul and his companions want to go to Asia but are kept from doing so by the Holy Spirit. They tried to go to Bithynia, but again the Spirit of Jesus said "Not yet, son." That night Paul had a vision and therefore headed to Macedonia and Europe. God has his purpose and keeping Paul and Peter the two leaders of the church, separated is probably part of that plan.

Later we realize that Peter is the apostle intended to go to Asia. He and the disciple John spent much time in that place. I remember as a young person with almost no ability, I was selected last to fill out a team. Others were very coordinated, even though I had the height. When we won games, it was not because of me but because God had selected a right team to do the job, and often it was not with me in leadership. I sat on the sidelines and listened to the coach, which was what I would be at Sheldon Jackson many years later. God is our leader and when the right time finally does come, it is wonderful to know that he has prepared the endeavor and that "Now it is your, turn, son," are wonderful words to hear.

"Gracious God, how often we think we know more than do you. We forget sometimes that you are in charge of not only the largest constellation in the heavens but also the small intricacies of feeling human beings and the proper and correct assigning of job and positions to them. Keep us in your will and we humbly attempt to do it. In your son's name we pray. Amen."

OLGOONIK INTERNATIONAL RACEWAY

"The Lord had said to Abram, 'Leave your country, your people and your father's household and go to the land I will show you. I will make you into a great nation and I will bless you; I will make your name great, and you will be a blessing. I will bless those who bless you, and whoever curses you I will curse; and all peoples on earth will be blessed through you.' So Abram left, as the Lord had told him; and Lot went with him. Abram was seventy-five years old when he set out from Haran."
Genesis 12:1-4

The sun is about fifteen degrees high in the sky, just to the back of the stands. It is just about midnight and we hear the words 10 - 9 - 8 - 7 - 6 - 5 - 4 - 3 - 2 - 1 -
"START YOUR ENGINES"
And they are off!

THE OLGOONIK INTERNATIONAL RACEWAY IS bounded on one side by the Arctic Ocean. It is bounded on the other side by a fresh water (in the summer time) lake and extends in one direction to the tundra and in the other direction to the tundra. In order to get the best traction possible the raceway is paved with gravel, and if there are a few graders, or would they be draggers, it is a fairly smooth track.

The vehicles that are warming up their engines at the present time are ATVs, which is translated All Terrain Vehicles, meaning that unless the surface is a lake or the ocean, they are supposed to go anywhere. In the winter when the tundra is frozen that may almost be the situation, but in the summer time when the tundra is translated into puddles, and deep holes, there are some places where the ATV cannot, or should not, go. The ATV is capable of racing along the shore of the ocean, but if a barrier is larger than a golf ball, traveling can be dangerous.

The race spectators are advised to look in one direction or the other, for swinging one's head 180 degrees in a constant manner is inadvisable. Those who are lying down in their beds are advised to use the pillows as ear plugs. If you are traversing the racetrack, it is advisable to look in both directions at the same time. This is possible because your ears will tell you which vehicle is the closest and therefore is the one to watch. There is no sexual barrier to racing in the event and some of the greatest racers are women.

As in all racing, the drivers are not going anywhere. The car that you presently see going in one direction will be the same car you see going in the opposite direction. The difference is which side of the driver's face that you see, which makes this kind of racing superior to the regular round-track racing where you only see one side of the driver's face.

Seat belts are advisable for the drivers because if the vehicle is thrown you will probably stay with the vehicle. However, the seat belt keeps the victor, and all who race are victors, from standing up for a victory lap. This is difficult to understand because when you stand your lap disappears.

Everyone is a winner as long as you stay on your side of the track, and this is not an English track. The length of the race depends upon the amount of fuel that you have on board and the endurance of the driver.

Ah, but the point of this parable is that the ATV drivers are going. Where, when and for how long has yet to be determined but they are going. I find that the entire human race is also going, not too sure just how long, or where or when they will arrive or if they will even know that they have arrived-but they are going.

And a sub-point of this parable is that the ATV drivers are on the track, or the main drag. Most of those in the rest of the world don't know if they are on track or not. Often they do not even care, they just want to be going. With the increase in the cost of petroleum products, more and more emphasis is being placed on knowing where you are going and trying to make as many errands count as you can because the next trip you make is going to cost you more.

An example of 'going' is found is our scripture reference. Things had been very comfortable for Abram, for all of his seventy-five years, and just when he should have been retired God gave him the greatest challenge of his life-GO. And all he told Abram was, "That when you get there I will let you know. You can't imagine what it will be like, therefore I won't bore you with details." So, Abram goes.

First he goes North and then he goes South and everywhere he goes he finds that there are many people before him. How is he going to carve out a 'promised land' when it seems to have been promised to hosts of other? But God has more than just trip insurance. He is planning on making everyone in the human family available to him for fellowship. First there will be many narrow places, some of which will be geographical. There may also be the insults of slavery to contend with, and there will be other narrow ways, legal, like as of laws that seem to favor the Israelites. There also will be worship, sort of a homing into the presence of God.

Ultimately, and Abram wonders if he is going to be part of it at this point, there will be a narrowing down to a single person, a messiah.

God didn't say that Abram might not be going all the way, but he is seeing the trip in the eyes of the people of Israel and Abram is just the engine at this point. The ATVs in Olgoonik may be on the way, but who knows just where they are going? Possibly some of those who feel the thrill of 'taking off' when they have come to the end of the track and are headed back in the opposite direction, will feel the thrill of really going on a trip that will greatly aid the community, and the Inupiat people. There have been great people in the past and we look for some great people in the future, but not just on the main-street-track.

So, I invite you to get off the Olgoonik track and get onto the main stream track. Go, but with a destination in mind. It may not be easy to see, but if you go God will ultimately guide you. A boat that is not moving cannot be steered, but a moving boat can, and often the steering device is a rudder hidden from view. May God bless you as you go to new places, to new challenges and possibly back here to Olgoonik to bring God's glory to your community.

"Gracious God give us the stamina to go and keep going, but also show us your will, and at your discretion the direction that you wish for us to go. We realize that many have gone before us, and we realize that we still have much time, but help us to make the most of that time. For we pray in your Son's name. Amen."

above

WEATHER - WEATHER - WEATHER
below

"The Pharisees and Sadducees came to Jesus and tested him by
asking him to show them a sign from heaven. He replied, When
evening comes, you say 'It will be fair weather, for the sky is red.'
and in the morning, 'Today it will be stormy for the sky is red
and overcast'. You know how to interpret the appearance of the
sky, but you cannot interpret the signs of the times. A wicked and
adulterous generation looks for a miraculous sign, but none will be
given it except the sign of Jonah:' Jesus left them and went away."
Matthew16:1-4

AT ANY ONE TIME, DAY or night, winter, spring, summer or fall, Alaska is a
mass of weather, and some feel that 'mass' should be spelled with an 'e'. If
someone comes from the lower forty-eight on an Alaska Airlines plane, they
have probably landed in the rain in Southeastern Alaska, in windy conditions
at Anchorage International Airport, possibly with ice fog or even clear weather
in Fairbanks, or with blowing snow in Barrow. They missed the fog of the
Aleutian peninsula and the always questionable weather on St. Lawrence
Island, via Nome. If they landed at Sitka, then they know how it is to land
on a postage stamp. Fortunately it is the commemorative size and the pilots
are excellent.

On their way to Olgoonik, pilots first have to determine if they can make it out of Barrow, and then whether or not the weather conditions are suitable for landing at Wainwright. It is also good to know what the weather is like en route and what to expect in case they have to turn back, to Barrow, or whether the Barrow field became closed in after you left.

Generally if you live in Southeastern Alaska and the weather is from the North, it will be clear and cold. If the weather is from the Southeast, then wet or snow is to be expected. Flying out the Aleutian chain the weather will be inclement, and that means real mean and bad, at least for flying.

Now if you plan on going by boat from Barrow to Olgoonik in the summer time or by snowmobile in the winter time, then it is also good to know whether storms are expected and how they will affect you. At Barrow the Beaufort and Chukchi Seas collide and there are strong currents that also affect the surface weather. Both of those seas are part of the Arctic Ocean.

There is a pass, north of Anchorage called Rainy Pass. For years the airlines had weather observers stationed in Rainy Pass so that they could radio the planes that were attempting to get through the pass as to what weather to expect. It was that important. Mind you, not just at one side of the pass but at both sides of the pass. The author has experienced several times a plane doing a 180 degree turn because the pilot "Couldn't see the other end of the passage." In Southeastern usually the pilot would find a calm bay and put the seaplane down for an hour and then try again. The weather changed that much, that often. With so much inclement weather the pilots flew VFR, "Visual Flight

Rules," "Can't see, don't go!" Weather is a fact of life and if you don't pay attention to it, it may mean the end of your life.

But notice in the title that there is also weather below weather. Here we refer to the ground, permafrost and also the resultant summer non-run off. The melted permafrost has no place to go, so it doesn't go anyplace.

The only foundation that is solid with respect to local Arctic villages is the permafrost, so you plan for it. If you build with normal foundation, cement etc. then when the heat of the building or the cement hits the ground the permafrost begins to melt. In many places in Southeastern Alaska the roads were built over muskeg, a spongy terrain. By laying slabs of wood and then pouring gravel on them the roads became passable.

In the Eastern Arctic during the winter the roads were formed by spraying layer after layer of water on the frozen tundra with a water truck. This made a solid road as long as it stayed frozen. When spring thaw came then the road was abandoned, the water from the ice helped the land turn green and they waited until the next fall before again building the road.

Most present day Arctic homes are built on pilings that rest on permafrost. For larger buildings, refrigeration units can be installed in the concrete which is then kept frozen during the warmer summer months. Some homes were built on a slab, which is what logging camps in Southeastern Alaska did in order to move the buildings when they moved to another stand of timber. In the Arctic a home, built on a slab is ready to move.

What has all this got to do with us? As the signs of the times, the weather is so very important to the Alaskan, and particularly to the villager who expects something for his survival to come on the next incoming plane or expects to leave on the outgoing plane for needed medical work There is an even more important fact found in the Scripture passage used for this parable.

In the Scripture passage Jonah was on his way to Ninevah, with the purpose of turning their attention to God. If he had had a billboard he would have warned the people and then the book of Jonah shows how he did not want to talk to the sinners in Ninevah because they might convert and then he wouldn't be able to see their destruction. Jonah was and stands as the patron saint of all who love to judge others. (If folks would spend more time worrying about heaven, rather than worrying about hell there might be more headed heavenward rather than hellbent.) So, we cannot do anything about changing the weather, well not very much, anyway, but we can do a lot about what the weather teaches us, the sign of Jonah.

Jonah never used his experience of being swallowed by the sea serpent as an evangelistic tool, he just had a simple message: "Turn from your simple, selfish ways where you have put yourself in the middle of everything, and give your attention to the will of God. God loves you, and he will continue to use you as you daily seek his will." It was the Old Testament version of Jesus Christ's New Testament statement, "God so loved the world that he gave his only son-for you." A sign of our times.

"Gracious God, who is full of grace, be with us as we struggle to bend our will in your direction, our attention to your word and our desires to that which you would desire for us. Give us momentary inspiration when we need guidance. Give us the basic solid love that will assist our loved ones and may the loved ones include all we come to know. In your son's name we pray. Amen."

TANIK

"Then the king will say to those on his right, 'Come, you who are
blessed by my Father; take your inheritance, the kingdom prepared for
you since the creation of the world. For I was hungry and you gave me
something to eat, I was thirsty and you gave me something to drink, I
was a stranger and you invited me in, I needed clothes and you clothed
me, I was sick and you looked after me, I was in prison and you came
to visit me.' . . . The king will reply, 'I tell you the truth whatever you
did for one of the least of these brothers of mine, you did it for me'"
Matthew 25:34-40

HOW DO YOU LIKE THAT?!?!?!? I have been a haole (Hawaiian) for a long time
and before that I was a cheechako, (Alaskan), a hen-ha (Japanese), and a
foreigner. For a while I also was a pelagi, (Samoan) and now I am a Tanik,
(Inupiat) a stranger, a foreigner.

It is strange, because at home I sing the same hymns that they sing here.
I use the same Bible that they use here, and I use the same Lord's prayer that
they use here. When it comes time for the doxology I sing the same words, or
possibly I sing different words but they mean, if translated, the same thing. I
praise the same God and I pray to the same God. When Jesus was on earth
he referred to God as his father and said that he is our father, also. If he is a
father to each of us then we are brothers and sisters. Being different cultures,
colors, nationalities, sizes, shapes, and a host of other "differences" God still
says that we are to be brothers and sisters. What is a brother or sister? One
who is part of the same family. But now I am a foreigner.

It is true that I do not have the same cultural past as the people who are
here in Olgoonik.

I remember going to a new high school in Pittsburgh, Pennsylvania where
I was different because almost all my other friends were black kids, but they
were good friends. I did not know that they were different until one day I
came in one of the side doors of the high school and one of the kids, a good
friend of mine said, "Smitty, that door is not for you." So I said, "Why? It
opens and I go through it." "Well," he said, "It is for the black kids and you
are a whitie." So I was a foreigner in my own high school.

Then I was playing with some of the kids in my neighborhood who happened to be Jewish. One of them got mad and said, "Ken, you are a foreigner, you are a gentile!" So I was a foreigner in my own neighborhood.

There are many walls that we can put up to keep ourselves in and also keep others out. But remember, if you build the wall you are the one that must break it down. If I try to break it down you will just get angry.

The word "tanik" is used often in Inupiat culture. Perhaps there is a secret in the English word, "tanic." Tanic sounds like tunic. The dictionary says that a tunic is:

A coat worn as part of a military uniform.

A gown-like outer garment worn by the ancient Greeks and Romans.

A woman's sleeveless upper garment usually extending down to her hips or below.

Possibly the secret to the tunic is that it is an attempt to hide who we really are, and that is where and when we become strangers. So if we are not to become or stay strangers it is necessary to become acquainted. In that way we can answer our question and solve our problems together, becoming true neighbors in the process.

Years ago I took a group of young people from the lower forty-eight into an Indian village in Southeastern Alaska. The streets were deserted, though we did have the feeling that the curtains on the windows were rustling a lot with no apparent breeze. A little later my group of youth was formally introduced to the community at the local church. It was a fun time, with lots of good food and lots of talking, a real communication. Many were invited into the local homes and there were lots of people on the street. They had been formally introduced.

Possibly we need to formally introduce the stranger, not just to explain who he is but who we are. Some of the questions that we might answer for both the strangers and also those who already seem to know each other are:

1. Your name, nickname and what family you have? Nicknames are easier to remember.
2. What you do in your village, or home community. What your job and hobbies are? What grade you are in school, your favorite subject and why?
3. Where you have traveled in the lower forty-eight and what were your experiences?
4. What are your personal hopes for the future and also for your community?
5. How active you are in your local church, either here in the village or in your home church?
6. What you will do for the rest of the summer? Or the year?

Some of these questions were asked in a group of visitors. Surprisingly many in the group of visitors did not know that information about the others with whom they were traveling, a trip of about three weeks time, up to Haines, on the boat trip and back down the Alcan Highway.

If we are going to be neighbors for eternity perhaps it is wise to begin finding out who we are and how we can be active neighbors right now and right here. The term 'tanik' hides a lot of important information that we need to know about each other, if we are going to be sisters and brothers of the faith.

I have often wondered how well-known the disciples were to each other, as they followed Jesus for three years. Certainly they knew the follies and the foibles and certainly there was some animosity, particularly when James and John seemed to assert their primary relationship. But did the disciples really spend time with each other? Yes, and therefore they came to know a lot about themselves. Likewise, Jesus knew a lot as he had the innate power of observation. We, too, can develop that power so that we can minister to those who feel the need but do not have the ability to express it.

May God bless us as we recognize the unique features that are in each one of us, not only because of our culture but because we are uniquely different, as God has so made us.

"Thank you God that I am who I am. That I have no duplicate and that I do not expect anyone to duplicate me. Help me develop into the person that you wish me to be. May my skills and my abilities be spent in worshiping you. I thank you that I can be me, with all that I have at your disposal. Give me strength for the daily journey and a vision of the ultimate purpose that you have for my life here on earth. For I pray in your son's name. Amen."

THE SMALL CHURCH AS JSF

"'How many loaves do you have?' he asked. 'Go and see.' When they found out, they said 'Five and two fish (telopia).' Then Jesus directed them to have all the people sit down in groups on the green grass. So they sat down in groups of hundreds and fifties. Taking the five loaves and the two fish and looking up to heaven, he gave thanks and broke the loaves. Then he gave them to his disciples to set before the people. He also divided the two fish among them all. They all ate and were satisfied, and the disciples picked up twelve basketfuls of broken pieces of bread and fish. The number of the men who had eaten was five thousand."
Mark 6:38-44.

COULD IT BE THAT JESUS missed the boat? He was preaching about the Kingdom of God, to an audience of 5000 men and about 4,500 women, along with probably a thousand or more youth and wow, what an audience. That was almost 10,000 people (with numbers I believe in being conservative, not liberal) and he held their rapt attention. This was his big chance to really spread the kingdom of God and he blew it. They must have been standing for he told the disciples to make them sit down, in groups of fifty or a hundred.

By then the disciples were a little shook. Where would they get enough food to feed this multitude? Jesus took the assets of the small boy, bread and fish, and gave thanks and when he distributed the food, lo and behold the people took the food they had brought in the *kophinos* (a small portable basket held under their robes) and they all had enough to eat. Then the disciples collected enough fragments to keep them for the next few days, putting them into their own *kophinos* and he dismissed the crowd.

What, no instructions for spreading the good news? No great parables that they would use to tell the good news? No great miracle of healing that they could talk about when they got home? How disappointing to one who would aspire to be bringing in the Kingdom of God, that would suffice for a short time, a long time and for eternity.

But let's look into the matter a little bit further. They would have sat down with people that they knew, from their own villages. They would talk about what Jesus had said (and the disciples would not be part of that conversation), and when they left they would trickle off to their own towns still talking about what they had heard. No one formally organized them so that some would be evangelists, some deacons, some elders, some Sunday School teachers and some women's study fellowship leaders.

What Jesus had done was to gather those who knew each other, who could support what they had heard by someone else who had heard the same thing. He energized them and they departed. Jesus used what our own military forces are now finding is the best way to wage a campaign, by using strike forces, small groups that have much in common and are trained to do the will of the commander.

They do not have the same capabilities, they have differing MOS numbers (Military Occupation Specialty, and we can change that to Mission Occupation Speciality) and they were a strike force. The more time they spent with the commander the easier it was to do what the commander would have wanted, ah, but still they checked in with the commander. Gideon also found it wise to use a small but loyal strike force and slowly, but surely, our military in the country are specializing in small strike forces.

As we have more and more people in the world, we are caught in the great battle of numbers. Our churches and their pastors talk about the great numbers of folk that they have in church, what a wondrous thing to preach to so many folk. When pastors are retired they still talk about the great numbers, but were those numbers a strike force or an audience? It is interesting that those retired ministers cannot remember the names of any of their members, and only a few on the sessions. As for the congregation, they have passed into oblivion.

Read the "Want ads" for church pastors and you see that the churches are still talking about the number of people in the congregation. If they had strike forces with that many people, they would need no pastors, or perhaps just one to calm them down and keep them from wearing themselves out.

Small churches are blessed to be a strike force in the communities in which we live. They do not have to worry about great organizational plans that really would require that everyone be on two or three committees in order to do the work of serving the community in the way that the community wants to be served.

If there is a need in the community, the person seeing the need calls a couple of other folks and they meet that need, solving the problem before many even know that it is a problem. They do not wait for a committee to be formed, for it to meet and enjoy refreshments. They don't write a plan of action or request funding from the appropriate ruling body, and then implement the plan of action. They don't write up a report stating what they did and how it could be improved in the future if there is another need to be met. The strike force, in the name of Jesus or his church reacts-and the problem is met and solved and life continues.

Note that Jesus divided the group, at their own direction, into small groups, he had a "kneel before the meal" (prayer before action) and allowed them to talk about anything that they wanted to talk about.

Thank God for a small church, even if we have to thank God by providing support for it. The Olgoonik church has spawned leaders such as Roy Ahmaogak and Sam Simmonds and George Agnasagga and who knows how many more. It is a wonderful place and it does not have to be divided into small groups, as there are not enough folks to divide.

Two members of the community can meet to talk about the community and the problems that they face with too many unloving people, but when they begin to talk about what God can do in such a situation they are the church, those who are concerned about what God is going to do with the people of the community. They are a JSF, a Jesus Strike Force.

Sometimes there a problem in a community that no one seems to care about or want to solve because it does not directly involve them. When two or three gather as a JSF they need to begin with prayer and talk it through, determining not what someone else should do but what they can do with the various abilities that God has spread throughout the group, or between just the two of them if that is all they are.

My wife and I visited Israel, and were put on a bus with fourteen black women from an Episcopal Church in New York City. Two other white folk got on the bus, saw the black folks and got off. Those two had a hard week, many were sick on their bus, they missed some of the sights and were miserable all the time. We kept seeing them at the various sites. There was a time when our black group was pushed out of the way for a group of white folk to go ahead. The black ladies smiled and said "That happens all the time, it makes no difference to us."

We had a wonderful time, the black ladies knew all the camp songs that we knew, and we sang them regularly. When we entered the Wailing Wall in Jerusalem, part of the old Temple, the guards were not going to allow us to enter, because we did not have a group and the black gals claimed us as their own. I got sick after leaving Masada and the gals took Betty while I recuperated and they had a wonderful time. We were blessed by the small group of which we became a part.

How fortunate we are to be part of a small church that is a JSF, a Jesus Strike Force.

"Loving heavenly father, we thank you for our church, which reminds us of the fact that UR is in the center of every c-h-ur-c-h. We thank you for the problems that we face for we recognize them as challenges for the future and for your kingdom. Help us to see the problems as challenges. Help us to be a JSF as we live in the community, that is Olgoonik or elsewhere. We recognize that both are your Church. In your son's name we pray. Amen."

THE CENTER OF OLGOONIK

"How lovely is your dwelling place, O Lord Almighty! My soul
yearns, even faints, for the courts of the Lord; my heart and my
flesh cry out for the living God. Even the sparrow has found a home,
and the swallow a nest for herself, where she may have her young - a
place near your altar, O Lord almighty, my King and my God."
Psalm 84:1-3

ONE OF THE PROBLEMS OF living within a remote Arctic village is that all
sorts of people want to examine how you are, what you do and how you relate
to those things which the tunics feel are necessities. Coming from modern
American culture they forget that your ancestors and their ancestors learned
how to live, enjoy and thrive in the Arctic clime. True they did not have
modern appliances which tend to weaken the body, mind and soul, but your
ancestors were a satisfied people and the culture that developed was well suited
to the locale and the environment in which they and you live.

The writer of the 84th Psalm indicates the feeling of belonging as he talks
of the dwelling place of God and his own satisfaction with living there.

Most students who come to study a remote Arctic village, who fortunately
for the community arrive and depart on the same day, want to find the center
of the community. They feel that from there they can move out to find, "All
there is to know'" about your culture, which usually is a smattering of what
you wish to share. So, where is the center of Olgoonik?

Those arriving would probably feel that the airport is the center. However
if they were typical, when the plane came to a stop the luggage was unloaded,
the new outbound luggage was loaded and the pilot left. He does not want
to be caught in an early arriving or late departing weather system so the less
ground time he or she has the better. There being no great administration
building we can count that out.

Those who are educationally inclined, and that is usually the group that
arrives, often feel that the school is the center of all activities. That is where the
young people are, though not always by choice, and that is where with luck
and a gracious teacher the students graduate, prepared for further education

as they are prepared by local folk for the hunting and fishing that will keep them alive and with a livelihood.

If you want to hear about the old days, then pay attention to the elders in the community. There is a new elderly building being built and by just sitting and listening, providing you can understand the language, you will hear how things were in the old days, or should I say the good old days.

You won't hear much over the roar of the ATVs out on the international drag strip, but that is where the teenagers are, along with those who have yet to graduate chronologically into or out or of the teenage livelihood. The TV and some radio stations from the 'outside' have affected them and they may appear to be a little more sophisticated than they really are, but so what is new, as that is the way teenagers are everywhere.

If you want to move inside, there is a teenage center and it is usually the place that they arrive at and depart from for other activities. They do have a good time though and their language is better understood by the examiners than by their own parents.

Of course, if you really want to know about the village take an elder and stroll through the cemetery. They will recount all those individuals there who died before their time, as most people do, and will tell of their exploits, and the usual foils and foibles.

In some way the elder with whom you are talking is sympathetic to, of and about those who he mentions, for he realizes that he is only a heartbeat away from lying six feet under in the permafrost, so he will want the next elder to be sympathetic to his life and actions.

Those who are politically involved are probably in the village corporation or possibly even in the borough. They will say that the borough or the village corporation is the center of the community for everything that is approved is approved by them. If you have a complaint, it better be good because they have heard every complaint in the world, such as too much noise at night.

There are three churches in this community of 500 people and those who are involved feel that in church is where you will get the true and accurate picture of who the village people really are. They also will have a relationship with folks in other villages and they will tell you of the wonderful singing, the wonderful pot luck meals (where everyone is lucky if you but attend) and will tell you of some of the famous folk who were members of possibly one of the local churches.

But, let's get serious. There is one place which probably can be called the center of town and that is the Olgoonik Hotel/Cafe. Here you see a healthy group of seniors, teenagers, housewives, day and night workers and anyone else in attendance. The staff sometimes act like bartenders in that they will listen and listen and wisely give no opinion, possibly just to nod of the head in an "I understand" knowing way. The food is excellent and there is no change required, everything comes out to even dollars. The lowest price is $ 1.00 and the main menu items are $10.00 regardless of what you order. There is very little, if any, local food but there are local names for other American-style fare.

It makes it handy for people like me who always look at the right hand side of every menu, which lists the prices. There is no need for change at all. They have a wireless internet so you can connect with your server and get all the news within seconds of its happening. This is indeed the center of the community, yet the servers act like the excellent waiters and waitresses that they are. There is no demonstrated pride, but rather a sense of this is where we can serve so we are serving.

So if a person lives in the community for two or three years, touching all facets of the social, physical and spiritual life, he or she will begin to understand the people who are good citizens of this far-out place, the center of their world. As a friend of mine once said of a rather far-out place, "This is the center of the world. From here I can go anywhere in the world, and I'm glad that I'm here!"

To go out of the village you go to Barrow. To head to Fairbanks or Anchorage, then you are really way out. To head into the lower forty-eight is unthinkable. Welcome to the community that we love.

"Gracious father, we thank you for the wonderful places that we live, here in Olgoonik or wherever we are placed on the planet earth. Bless our neighbors and those with whom we share our lives. May the peace that you give surround us, in spite of the whirling noise of civilization or the peaceful noise of the gulls and sea animals. In your son's name we pray. Amen."

THE CAKEWALK

"Who shall separate us from the Love of Christ? Shall trouble or
hardship or persecution or famine or nakedness or danger or sword?
No, in all these things we are more than conquerors through him
who loved us. For I am convinced that neither death nor life, neither
angels nor demons, neither the present nor the future, nor any powers,
neither height nor depth, nor anything else in all creation, will be able
to separate us from the Love of God that is in Christ Jesus our Lord."
Romans 8:35, 37-39

IT IS AMAZING HOW THINGS change with the changes in society. The original
meaning of a cake walk was, "A musical promenade of black American origin
where a cake was given to the couple who demonstrated the most unique
and imaginative dance figures and step." It was awarded to you when you
spiraled and slid your partner across the dance floor. In some cases, the name
was given to other facets of this dance, if you strutted, ambled or improvised
a particular style when you dipped, swung, plunged, whatever. But there is
another American version of the cake walk, one that played an important part
in early American history.

In this cake walk, various cakes were made and then divided into two
different classifications. In pioneer America the mother would bake a cake
and her children would watch her mix the batter, then the wonderful smelling
cake came out of the oven. Some of the kids licked the pan, after it cooled
and others watched while mother put icing on the cake using a butter-sugar
frosting and adding all sorts of twirls, ridges and any inventive decoration she
could add, providing it was made out of the icing mixture.

At the cakewalk adventure the cakes of all the mothers were put on a
table and then people bid for the cakes as a fund raising event. The children
would not tell which one their mother had made, but as the prices went up
the children would ohhh, and ahhh and their eyes would open wide at the
money that people were paying for their mother's cake. The winner of the cake
almost always invited the children to have a slice, the mother was gratified
and the children were more than gratified They were excited and the money
raised went to a good cause. But - - -

There was another purpose. The single girls, probably of a marriagable age, would also bake their cakes and then frost them with even more intricate swirls peaks and sometimes figures in icing. They really decorated their personalities into the frosting of the cakes. Some even made the icing thicker so that you got almost as much icing as you did cake.

They placed their cakes on a separate table, reserved just for them. These cakes had a purpose. The single fellows (who were not allowed to see the cakes before hand) would then bet on the cakes and with the cake went the baker. When you bought a cake the baker, who would identify herself only at the end of the cakewalk went with the cake. So began a relationship that often ended up in marriages and so the term, "The marriage was just a piece of cake." A lot of psychology strategy was involved, though they did not call it that, in getting the cake of someone that you were really interested in. If you wanted a farmer's wife, then you looked for the solid cake that would give a man enough energy to go out and milk the cows before bedtime. If the icing on the cake was frilly then possibly your woman would be the frilly one, and if it was a sedate decoration then you probably would get a homebody. It was a hilarious time and your sweet-heart was really a result of a sweet taste.

Let's now move into an Arctic village where we are going to have another cakewalk. This event is also a fund raiser, but in a community that is often without money. Money is a scarcity, where many things are done with no financial remuneration and other jobs often are taken by tuniks thereby reducing the funding ability of the resident population. The cake walk includes possibly pies and also small bits of candy.

When there is a death in the family much can be done with volunteers; the preparing of the funeral service; the digging of the grave in the permafrost which often means hammering out the pieces of frozen gravel and getting enough gravel to again fill the grave at the end of the funeral; and transportation for the family, when the family does not have a car. The casket must be flown in, probably from Barrow, and there are other financial necessities. Often the family cannot afford to fly a coffin in so local carpenters will create the box and only after the funeral is over will they screw in the top of the box prior to burial.

The cakewalk is the solution. Tickets are sold, possibly twenty for a dollar. When enough tickets have been sold then a winning ticket is selected, possibly for a prize of a portion of the candy. A person can buy more tickets to be added to the pot at any time and often the feeling is that a recent ticket will rise to the top of the pot and be drawn. The cakewalk continues until all the candy is finally gone, the pies or the cakes have been sold and the family has been helped to finance what was an unexpected and seemingly impossible expense.

The funeral is held, and the body is laid to rest in what will be a permanent freeze. The family and neighbors usually end the evening with a sing-spiration in the local church, the same one from which the person was buried, and the sing-spiration can extend into the wee hours of the morning.

The cake walk also becomes an opportunity to celebrate an individual's life, and the sorrow of the passing is assuaged by the wonderful melody and harmony of Eskimo voices. So it has been for many years, and it is truly a satisfying time in the life of the community.

We need to find other opportunities for expressing our grief. It is not uncommon in our modern society to 'drown' our sorrows by the use of drugs and alcohol. This usually adds more grief to an already grieving family. The cakewalk provides for the family of the deceased and at the same time joins the family in the celebration, and loss, of a life that is very important in the community.

"Loving heavenly father, we thank you for your son and the promise of eternal life with you that guides us in our daily lives. We thank you for the saints who have gone to their eternal relationship with you and we look forward to rejoining them in worship of you. May our lives show that faith as we mix and mingle with those around us. Make us mindful of our temporality on earth, but also our eternity with you. For we pray in your son's name. Amen."

MY LIFE AS A GOPHER

"By the grace God has given me, I laid a foundation as an expert
builder, and someone else is building on it. But each one should
be careful how he builds. For no one can lay any foundation
other than the one already laid, which is Jesus Christ. If any
man builds on this foundation using gold, silver, costly stones,
wood, hay or straw, this work will be shown for what it is,
because the Day will bring it to light. It will be revealed with
fire, and the fire will test the quality of each man's work."
I Corinthians 3:10-13

AS A BOY I HELPED my father repair our car, work on the house, build a new
garage and make other changes in our environment. He was the mechanic
and builder and I was the go-fer. He would say, "The phillips head screw
driver," and I would go-for it. He would say, "The cross cut hand saw," and
I would go-for it.

Several times in college and soon after when we were building a log
church and an educational unit I was not only the go-for but had graduated
to the digger. The foundations were dug into blue clay that had one time been
ocean bottom. I would stand on the shovel until I had a shovelful of blue clay
and then toss the shovel and the blue clay out of the hole. Then someone would
scrape it clean, douse the shovel in water and then throw it back to me while
I had dug another shovel full of blue clay. The foundation was solid, concrete
on subterranean blue clay.

We were also aware of the need for insulation and a vapor barrier. In
Alaska, insulation was put between the inside and outside walls. The insulation
had a vapor barrier on it for there was much water, and depending on the
heat in the building the vapor pressure pushed the moisture into or out of
the structure. When building with logs we left a four-inch space between the
logs and caulked it with plumber's ookum, inside and outside, leaving the
four inches of space there to stop the air, but at the same time to allow the
vapor pressure to go between the logs. Otherwise the logs would experience
early rot.

We also were involved in building in Hawai'i. Not only were the foundations deep, but we also had single wall construction with electrical outlets in the door posts because the walls were not thick enough to handle the light fixture and switches. We also used clips that would join the rafters and the walls. When you have been in a hurricane you know that is necessary. Although there were many differences in how the structures were built I would still go-for things that people needed to build.

We had returned to the central part of Alaska, but concerned with the Arctic slope. We knew that good construction meant that you must have solid foundations and that permafrost was that solid foundation material. That meant that you dug into the permafrost and put in pilings on which the building would rest.

The house generates heat and that heat can melt the permafrost and thereby ruin your foundations, so the pillings have to be deep enough to be imbedded in the cold of the permafrost. Some commercial buildings have refrigerants in their base wall so that there will be no changing of temperature when a temporary thawing of the permafrost takes place. No amount of jacking up the building and inserting boards or rocks or any other substance will take the place of a permanent hard foundation.

Now let's move into theology for a moment. I am disturbed by how many sects, cults and other religious stratifications manage to build what seems to be a strong theology. They have writers, usually only one per religion who writes what he or she feels is a strong statement of their interpretation of religion. Sometimes they quote the Bible and sometimes they paraphrase the Bible, but never do they duplicate the Bible.

The foundation of the Christian faith is the statement of belief that Jesus Christ is the only son of God and that he came to earth to be Lord of mankind and to show mankind what God is like. A person who accepts Christ as savior is a Christian person, regardless of how often or how seldom he or she worships. There is no other foundation of the faith, no individual, no pleasant sayings, no good deeds done. In the Greek the foundation is rock, *petra,* and every time it is used in Scripture it refers to Jesus the Christ. The Greek words are the closest words that we have to the original sayings of Jesus. In our Scripture passage for this parable Paul is very succinct in his statement the Jesus Christ is the Foundation of our faith. To accept anything else means that you have to shore up the foundation, keeping it shifting so that the shifting theology of the religion seems stable.

In a period where there is freedom of religion, and even freedom from religion, there is a tendency to accept all religions as equal. Such cannot be. I find it difficult to be ecumenical with a faith that would denigrate my God, and make him less than he is. I can remember only one time in my life when

I was instructed to build something in order to blow it up. That was during practice for the Army demolition of enemy buildings, and we had to build them to destroy them. I can accept no statement of God that says that he created mankind so that he could destroy him.

God seeks for all men to come to him, regardless of what culture they find themselves in, to honor and glorify him and to live the life that the son, Jesus the Christ lived. We then are ready for an eternity with him in a true fellowship where we accept God as the ultimate authority, his words being Our Word, and his son being our Lord and master.

"Gracious God we want to be honest with you and with ourselves. We are positively convinced that you are God and that we will serve you with our lives here on earth and wherever we might go. Help us to understand that which we can in order to live as honestly as possible with you, now and through eternity. In Jesus's name we pray. Amen."

EMPTY PILINGS

"Precious in the sight of the Lord is the death of his saints. O
Lord, truly I am your servant; I am your servant, the son of your
maidservant; you have freed me from my chains. I will sacrifice a
thank offering to you and call on the name of the Lord. I will fulfill
my vows to the Lord in the presence of all his people, in the courts of
the house of the Lord - in your midst, O Jerusalem. Praise the Lord."
Psalm 116:15-19

BEFORE CONTINUING I'D SUGGEST THAT the reader look up the 116th Psalm
and read it all the way through. Then note that this is before the 117th Psalm,
the shortest chapter of the Bible, that the 118th Psalm is the middle book of
the Bible and that the 119th is the longest book of the Bible.

We have done a lot of traveling in Alaska. Just about everywhere we
have seen the presence of pilings that no longer have structures on them. The
pilings were driven either down and into the permafrost, into the ocean
bottom if they were over water, or through the muskeg and into the hard
surface beneath.

In some cases the pilings were just on top of rock for that was the *petra*,
the durable foundation which of course in the Christian Faith is the belief
in Jesus the Christ as being God's son. As I mention empty pilings there are
loads of individuals of whom I am reminded, persons who lived their faith
and affected many others because of their actions and words. There are many
places in Alaska that remind me of Christian folk who were grounded in the
Christian Faith, and whose witness still endures even though the human
structure (the physical person) on the piling is no long present. Still, their
'grounding in faith' is very present.

Note that in the Bible passage the word for saint is never capitalized. In
many cases they were more saintly than some of those, or all of those who
have been canonized but within the Protestant tradition all believers are saints
and none of us is capitalized. The pilings represent what is left of many saintly
organizations or ministries within the state of Alaska, possibly within the
last hundred or two hundred years, and admittedly they will be Presbyterian
oriented or instigated.

Dr. Sheldon Jackson early realized that the Presbyterian denomination could not evangelize the entire state by itself, so the comity agreement was made with other cooperating denominations. This divided the work amongst those denominations that would cooperate. For the most part they have continued to cooperate in what is not only a good administration of Christian effort to the state, but also what is a wonderful Christian fellowship.

There are also other ministries that were or are not immediately of the Presbyterian Church. Many have taken part in cooperative ministry where the integrity of the witness was a genuine sharing of theological differences but within the context of Christian love. Dr. Jackson saw that there was need for good education for all youth in the state and therefore not only Sheldon Jackson School was begun, but he also worked to bring good education to the entire state. Dr. Jackson also realized the difficult plight of the Eskimo folk who had their game driven further away than they could go so he was involved in bringing reindeer to the state, several years in a row, until finally the United States Government acceded to help finance the venture. Later also Rev. R. Rolland Armstrong, nicknamed Army, took part in the Alaska Constitutional Convention, the only minister to do so, and helped write the present state Constitution.

The empty pilings mentioned here represent the attempt to meet the spiritual needs of the folk of Alaska, both native and white, and will be listed in no particular temporal or geographical order. Many of them are related to other programs and in each case the local church or churches were supportive of or totally involved in their efforts.

1. Flying ministry, with pilot-pastors John Chambers and Bill Wartes. Flying in the most difficult weather in the world the planes not only carried missionaries, but also medical cases to hospitals. They also carried food and building material to isolated communities, or should I say ice-olated communities. With the advent of heavier use of commercial bush pilots the ministry did not survive, but many owe their lives and their church buildings to the flights made by the Arctic Messenger, the name of the plane.

2. Hospitality House. Realizing that Eskimo girls coming from native villages did not understand the larger cities into which they were coming, Mable Rasmussen established Hospitality House in Fairbanks. Here the girls were given health checkups and introduced to the white man's ways of doing things and thinking. Mable was, and always will be, remembered as a mother to not only the resident girls but also others who came to her for assistance. There are many of those women who have now returned to their homes in the villages but who remember with love the attention of Mable.

3. At her retirement from Hospitality House, Mable Rasmussen began and carried through a ministry with the jails and correctional institutions.

She knew the villages from which many of them came and she lavished the same attention on inmates that she did on those girls who had come from the villages to Hospitality House. Many a man and woman has gone "straight" because Mable smoothed the transition from correctional institution to main stream living.

4. Bert Bingle and his ministry along the Alcan Highway and the Alaska Railroad. He was a man who was always serving his congregation, hopping off a slow freight or driving for a couple of hours and then taking a 'Bingle'-a ten minute nap and back on the road. He served road crews, Indian folk, railroad workers and anyone else who needed anything. His car normally carried a trunk load of fish, and the back seat was full of things that had been left by those who preceded him along the highway.

5. Haines House where children had more than just a second chance. If some youth had not been accepted in his own hometown, he or she was accepted at Haines House. In some cases this also led to the person attending Sheldon Jackson School particularly when it was a high school.

6. Chukotka Native Association, linking those Yupic Eskimo folk with their distant cousins in Eastern Siberia, together holding worship services both in Alaska and also in Russia. There was also an exchange between other Alaskan congregations and their Russian Orthodox spiritual brothers and sisters in Russia. This emphasis was aided by the Russian speaking Rev. Willa Roghair, pastor of the church in Barrow.

7. Sheldon Jackson School, Junior College and College which was active in the educating of young people both native and white from the Southeastern, Interior and Arctic Slope areas of Alaska. Superintendents Leslie Yaw and Orin Stratton, Dean Roland Wurster and teachers Gladys Whitmore and Jim Robinson stand out as luminaries in the darkness of an Alaskan winter. Only recently the pilings have come to light as they seek to continue in some way the ministry, particularly to Alaska Native folk through some viable kind of ministry. Possible spin offs have been the Alaska Native Brotherhood and the Sisterhood, the Alaska Federation of Natives and Presbyterian assistance in the Land Claim Bill. Whenever there was a need that the secular part of society would not assist, then the church came in to pave the way for positive reparation.

8. The Motor Vessel Anna Jackman Ministry, formerly the Princeton Hall, ministered to logging camps, light house personnel and others who lived in the remote areas of Southeastern Alaska. A summer ministry involved Vacation Bible Schools and also Go-See Seminars and the transporting of Volunteer In Mission groups. Active were captains Ed Cade, Dick Nelson, Laurie Doig and ministers Dick Stussi, Ward Murray and Bill Zeiger.

9. Various executives with their particular style effected change of the churches from Mission Outposts to self-determining churches. J. Earl Jackman, with the little black book, Army Armstrong, Bill Pritchard, Gordon Corbett and Neal Munro battled inclement weather, isolation and meager resources as they led the church.

10. Others had their emphases with Mayreld (Swanson) Parker as the Christian Education specialist; Neal Kuyper with his counseling assistance; Jim Simpson who could squeeze Christian Education out of a turnip, and Ralph Weeks who flew in ministry to several Arctic villages.

11. There are a multitude of pastors and individual church leaders who have been the 'infantry' in the spiritual warfare. They and the lay folk have been involved in multitudes of meetings, in volunteer building of physical and spiritual buildings, in prostitute rehabilitation, food banks, alcohol counseling, homeless shelters and other valued community emphases. In most of these efforts the needs are still being met.

All of these institutions and persons were rooted in the Love of God expressed through various means. The responsibility has now been passed on to us to continue what at one time was a very apparent ministry. Much of their life and training has been integrated into our own witness and the responsibility is now in our hands to make a good witness to the love of God which is not something hidden but something seen. We are saints.

"How can I repay the Lord for all his goodness to me? I will lift up the cup of salvation and call on the name of the Lord. I will fulfill my vows to the Lord in the presence of all his people." The same Psalm, just the 12th through the 14th preceding verses.

This precedes the 117th Psalm, the shortest chapter in the Bible which reads, "Praise the Lord, all you nations; extol him, all you peoples (and that includes all of us) For great is his love toward us, and the faithfulness of the Lord endures forever. Praise the Lord."

"Gracious God we can forget the buildings, physical and spiritual, we can forget the pilings, those individuals and groups that were grounded in the faith, but we will never forget the Love of God expressed in the life, death and resurrection of Jesus the Christ, your son. Gracious God, help us to remember. In your son's name we pray. Amen."

OLGOONIK THE FAVORED CITY

"For here we do not have an enduring city, but we are looking for
the city that is to come. Through Jesus, therefore, let us continually
offer to God a sacrifice of praise - the fruit of lips that confess his
name. And do not forget to do good and to share with others, for
with such sacrifices God is pleased. Obey your leaders and submit
to their authority. They keep watch over you as men who must
give an account. Obey them so that their work will be a joy, not a
burden, for that would be of no advantage to you. Pray for us."
Hebrews 13:14-18a

THERE ARE MANY THINGS THAT make Olgoonik a favored city. It is part of the
North Slope Borough, a borough being like a county in the lower forty-eight.
There are sixteen boroughs in Alaska and though they cover the populated
areas, those areas of the state that are not included in a borough are controlled
by the state. The services the city cannot or will not provide are provided by
the borough.

Olgoonik is also composed of people who are predominantly of the
same cultural heritage, Inupiat. There may be others but the Inupiat culture
is dominant. Cultural traditions have been carried along from generation to
generation and the people now live within the legal relationships of the state
of Alaska, in the United States of America. It is necessary to say this as there
are some Indian or cultural groups in the United States that claim to not be
American, though they are not within Alaska.

These independent cultural groups call themselves a different nation, and
there are still other groups attempting to gain this independent-native-status.
They still are immediately adjacent to the United States and expect all the
benefits that an American citizen has, but are themselves desirous of being a
different nation, often with differing social, moral, ethical and legal status.

The city of Olgoonik has very modern equipment with both water and
sewer lines buried underground in insulated tubes. The water-making plant
is huge and there is an electricity generating power plant sufficient for the
entire city. There are no rural areas in Olgoonik. No one lives, nor could
they exist, outside the city limits. The land is just barren tundra. Almost

everything operates with fuel oil. Fuel oil and gasoline are shipped in once a year on barges that bring millions of gallons. There are only three stores, two grocery stores and the Olgoonik Walrus Café, and they are run by managers appointed by the city council. No private commercial store could make a go of it here because the transportation costs would kill their efforts and there could never be any competition with the village.

There is only one service station that handles gasoline for cars, small trucks, boats, snow machines or ATVs. The village corporation owns everything so there is no competition. Because of this the Barrow radio station that is most listened to has no commercials, only public service announcements. Everything in Olgoonik runs on Eskimo time, often weather-dependent. If there is a schedule, you would have to listen consistently for a year to figure out what it was or is, and by then it probably would change several times.

Disturbingly, Olgoonik flies people in from the lower forty-eight to service all the equipment. It is interesting that they don't have three or four local men who are mechanically inclined learn how to service the equipment. To fly someone in at salary, travel, board and room is puzzling when there are so few monetary salaried jobs in town anyway.

Everything is paid for by the oil/gas money that is paid to the borough. One wonders what will happen when the oil money runs out, not if but when. Of course the city and the borough are all for additional drilling.

There is not a lot of landscaping. Although there is no snow at the present time, this is being written on the longest day of the year, the 21st day of June, when the winter closes in (and tomorrow the days will begin getting shorter until the 21st of December), landscaping is not really important.

But, tomorrow the daylight time will be shorter, by just a few seconds and the day after possibly a minute and on and on and everyone knows it. There is a psychological factor in knowing that summer, though it is just beginning, is going to terminate in fall and that will terminate on the shortest day of the year.

Just a few days beyond that 21st of December date is the celebration of Christmas. Therein lies a secret. Possibly the greatest problem with things now is that there is not a problem with things now. Everything is taken care of financially. There is just so much stuff that you can have in one's home. Magazines, newspapers and DVDs will stir within you a desire for more of the world's good, but it won't happen unless you leave Olgoonik, and Olgoonik is home.

Those who have served time in jail admit that everything is taken care of with respect to their living conditions. A place to sleep, eat and play music or TV, and the only problem is that they are not free.

There are some who do not take easily to the religious expression that they know because they are not free to choose. You do exactly what that religious expression says or you will be lost, condemned so you are not free.

The 21ˢᵗ of December is followed in a few days by the 25ᵗʰ of December. It is more or less the accepted date of the birth of Jesus. We will not dispute the date. The fact is that God, who has provided all the things that we observe in the tangible world with possessions piled upon more possessions, has also provided an opportunity for there to be a spiritual relationship.

Now, that is free.

You have the free choice to accept the gift that God has given or to reject him. Look at the scripture for this parable, both in light of the present community of Olgoonik and also as an eternal Olgoonik. At the present time those who have rejected the gift are in the majority. But it does not need to be so.

The secret is that when things are the darkest, God has provided his son to make things better or brighter. It was no accident that Jesus claimed to be the light of the world. Lots of people burn candles to represent Jesus. I would prefer that they burn 100 watt lights because Jesus is not a slim flickering glow, but a bright and shining example of what the real human life can be. That leads to the true spiritual life. Isn't it strange that with all the local emphasis on spirituality that the term is not used in the New Testament, and in a sense used almost derogatively in the Old Testament. The spiritual ones, Scribes, Pharisees and Saducees were the ones that gave Jesus most of his trouble.

God the Father and God the Son want us to accept the Holy Spirit also, not for personal sanctification but to accomplish God's will in the world. Olgoonik depends upon oil. In the future it may have to depend upon methane gas the mass of gas to be found beneath the earth. and below the city.

For the Christian the energy to do God's will, and the direction that one needs to take to accomplish God's will, will always come from God. But the real secret to life is a relationship with God who created the earth, the Inupiat and the taniks.

"Gracious God, forgive us for seeing only half of all that you have created, that is the physical. We seek to understand the spiritual life that you also have created. We recognize that we will leave the physical behind at the point of death yet the spiritual relationship will continue. We do not desire to have spirituality, but rather to be the persons that you would have us become. We thank you for Jesus your son, in whose name we pray. Amen."

WHALING CAPTAIN

"Then the word of the Lord came to Jonah a second time: 'Go
to the great city of Nineveh and proclaim to it the message I give
you.' Jonah obeyed the word of the Lord and went to Nineveh. The
Ninevites believed God. They declared a fast, and all of them, from
the greatest to the least, put on sackcloth. When God saw what they
did and how they turned from their evil ways, he had compassion
and did not bring upon them the destruction he had threatened."
Jonah 3:1,2,5,10

THE POSITION OF WHALING CAPTAIN is a difficult position to attain. Normally
the captain has served as an apprentice on ships in many different places. He
has served as the one who steers the boat, as the harpooner, and as the one
who ties the whale to the boat but can slip the knot if the whale sounds. The
captain must know all the positions, and when it comes to forming a whaling
crew he has to put the best persons in the determined places. In an emergency,
the probability is that the men will sacrifice themselves in order to catch a
behemoth of blubber.

It is necessary for the Captain to check the boat as soon as the last snows
of winter pass. He makes sure the ribs are strong, the seams still tight in spite
of the winter snow and whether all the rope is in good condition. A rope
that breaks with the whale on its attached harpoon is a disgrace. The captain
is more than just a sportsman. He is making sure that the village has meat
for the coming winter. He is also the object of prayers in the local church,
for village subsistence depends upon his skill and his decisions. Probably he
should introduce a member of the family to his crew, but he also wants to
represent the different families with persons of his family on his crew.

The captain determines whether the whales are near or not. He makes the
decision to pursue a whale that is spotted. The crew can make suggestions but
he is the one to make the decision.

His actions will be the subject of discussion by the elders who sit around
tables in their waning years, and a wise decision or one that determined
that the village would have meat is a reputation that he lives with. He is not
Jack or Ezekiel or Jeremiah but is rather called "Captain" and that title will

stay with him as long as he is in the village. If there is any hero worship in the village, the "Captain" will be the one getting it. Movie stars, basketball figures, baseball and football heros mean almost nothing for the village does not live or die because of them.

Because the whaling captain is an important person, his judgement is often sought on other village issues. Probably he will be on the city corporation board when there is another vacancy. His wife, who was just another girl in her family now is the one who is married to the Captain. She is elevated in status, but they do not always show it.

Though there is minor competition in whaling, the needs of the city come first. There have even been times when one village could not get any whales, because the whales just did not come close to the village. Then another village 'Took' a whale for the other village, with no bragging about the feat.

When the waling captain decides that the season is over he pulls his boat up on the village beach, turns it over and the crew is finished. If another whale shows, up his crew can help those who might still be out, but usually his boat is finished for the season.

The whaling captain has learned much from those who have gone before. He has to be willing to take suggestions and then evaluate them within the light of the present situations. It is not a sport fishing situation. The life and death of the community depends on his abilities, and how eager he is to be about his business. He may have any number of jobs in the community when the whaling season is not in force, but those are all put aside when the season begins.

William Ernest Henley was a famous poet, who died in 1903. Still more famous were the poets and writers that he promoted so that their work would be known by the world: Kipling, Wells, Yeats and Robert Louis Stevenson. Henley did not become famous but he did write much good verse. Possibly his best loved poem was <u>Invictus</u>.

> Out of the night that covers me,
>   Black as the Pit from pole to pole,
> I thank whatever gods may be
>   For my unconquerable soul.
> In the fell clutch of circumstance
>   I have not winced nor cried aloud.
> Under the bludgeonings of chance
>   My head is bloody, but unbowed.
>
> Beyond this place of wrath and tears
>   Looms but the Horror of the shade,

And yet the menace of the years
  Finds and shall find me unafraid.

It matters not how strait the gate,
  How charged with punishments the scroll,
I am the master of my fate:
  I am the captain of my soul.

As human beings created by God, we have the right to the philosophy of Invictus, and even though we are unconquerable, we can determine to put our lives and our souls into the hand and experience of God and accept his authority. As Christians, we become whaling captains and instead of seeing pits, bludgeonings, horror, menace and punishments we give our whaling captain lives to God for his use.

The rest of the world will see us and regardless of the words or actions they will give the glory to God the Father. It is up to us to make sure that our lives are consistent with God's desires. Our relationship with Jesus Christ makes that possible.

As we pick our crew, those friends, business associates and social contacts with whom we will be going through life, we should be aware that they each have special abilities that God can use, especially their abilities to share themselves with us in a spirit of concern. Our concern is not just for ourselves but for the entire human community and we must be alert to being readily available to any call from the ultimate captain, God.

God knows what is best and we will be happiest when we follow his will. There is one guarantee. There is almost nothing more exciting than the anticipation of the whaling experience, the run out of the boat on the ice, the chase with the boat, the strike with the harpoon, the drag of the struggle and then the awaited anticipation of the village when the whale is dragged ashore for butchering.

The only thing more exciting is the daily life of the Christian in meeting new and unexplained challenges and responding with resources that you did not think that you had, always under the guidance of God who has created all of existence, carried you along with his will to experience an eternity with him, with the 'Communion of the saints' always in the audience.

"Loving heavenly father, each of us was a child, but each of us has grown. Take our backgrounds, our beginnings, our lives and use us to honor and glorify yourself. We do not know the sum total of our abilities, nor the extent of our days but with the life that we have we give ourselves to you. Use us in your will, for in anticipation we pray in Jesus's name. Amen."

ULU

"For the word of God is living and active, sharper than any double-edged sword, it penetrates even to dividing soul and spirit, joints and marrow; it judges the thoughts and attitudes of the heart. Nothing in all creation is hidden from God's sight. Everything is uncovered and laid bare before the eyes of him to whom we must give account."
Hebrews 4:12, 13

KNIVES ARE VERY IMPORTANT TO the Eskimo hunter and also his wife. Because hunting is the way of life, and because the entire animal is used--blubber, meat, skin, bones and intestines--it means that skill with a knife is necessary for the man or woman. Once the animal or fish is killed, skinning or separating the hide from the body of the animal is necessary. The knife used most often by the women for this job is an ulu, though men also are skilled in its uses.

The ulu has a flat fan-shaped blade with a grip in the center of the opposite side. Though it has become a very popular tourist article, it is a picture of skill to watch an Eskimo woman use the knife with a slightly circular motion to easily and accurately separate the skin from the meat of the animal, saving as much of the animal as possible.

Probably the first used ulus were made of slate so that they could keep their sharpness. The modern ulu is made of up-to-date metal, is ultra sharp and is a necessity in an Eskimo kitchen. It is also popular with tourists. The tourist item is made from baleen or metal but because they are knives they are not allowed in carry-on baggage on the airlines.

Interestingly it is a utensil that folks in the lower forty-eight have found useful, and whether used with a chopping block or used in regular food preparation ulus are becoming more plentiful.

Though there may be the word "ulu" in Africa there is probably only one other language where the "ulu" is a very important part of the language, and that is Hawaiian. The Hawaiian definition of ulu is:

1. To grow, increase, spread; grove, growth, collection; an increase or rising of the wind or an increase, such as in the surf.

2. Possessed by a spirit; inspired by a spirit, god, ideal, person; stirred; to enter in and inspired, to stir up, inspire or excite.

The second definition leads to the scripture passage that leads this parable, and that is that the Bible, the Word of God, is a sharper ulu than a two edged sword.

There are many things that do not pertain to life, and books that do not stir the imagination, but merely present a plot. When finished they can be forgotten with ease. There are some issues that do not warrant further discussion. And then there are some items that warrant so much further discussion that they are always mentioned in conversations, particularly for those who are growing in their own thinking.

The two-edged sword mentioned in the scripture was kept in a scabbard, normally on the left-hand side of the warrior. In battle, its owner reached across his body from the right-hand side to grasp the sword and he was then ready for battle. He also kept a dagger or knife on his right -hand side for ease of grasping it. The sword was used to either stab or dismember the opponent, and the sharper the sword the faster the opponent was killed. Like the sword, the Bible, is an ulu that penetrates even to dividing the spirit and the soul. The soul is that which will continue with God at the time of death.

Religionists often seek to count the number of souls that they have saved, forgetting that it is the entire person for whom they were responsible. Early missionaries would often make that distinction. The spirit is the life of the individual because without spirit, breath, the body did not live and without the spirit the soul does not live.

As the sword is to be always ready for action, so should our awareness of God's Word be always at the ready. It is not necessary to memorize long portions of it, but it is necessary to know what is contained in the Bible, the long eternal length love song that God has for each individual.

It is also good to know that the Holy Spirit will come to a person's aid when he or she needs revelation from God's Word. Having studied the Bible there will be times when just the right answer comes at the right time. That only happens, though, when the Bible is kept at 'ready'.

The sword of God also divides the joints and the marrow, and one is reminded of this when a wife prepares the meat for roasting, cutting away that part which will not be tasty but leaving the full meat.

The ulu example of the Bible is that it lays bare before the eyes of God the thoughts and the attitudes of the heart. If your attitude of the heart and mind is one of love for your fellow man, an agape love not a sensual love, then your words and thoughts and actions will reveal that attitude. This must be the honest attitude of the heart of the person because God sees everything, not just the apparent things.

We have experienced entering a room and realizing that there is one picture on the wall that is not hanging straight. We feel embarrassed to see it, and we want to change it so that it is also perpendicular with the walls and the ceiling but it is not our room, but a friend's. There may be eighteen or twenty pictures that are hung properly but we forever remember that room because one of the pictures is not hanging straight. So it is with God.

Your actions may seem to be perfectly in line with his will, up and down and across but that one picture, habit, foul language, lie, or stretching of the truth still sticks out and reminds you that all is not well. It is a real joy when the owner of the room moves over and straightens the picture and remarks how much better the room is with everything hanging as it should, and you feel better when you confess before God the strained relationship and know that he has forgiven you.

God sees the attitudes of our hearts and realizes that there are still a few things in our lives that are not quite in his will. It is easier to pray when the room of our lives is in order.

So it is that the Bible, the ulu of God's word, straightens up many things in our lives. That means that constant Bible study, Sunday School and Worship are necessary to retrain our lives so that they are in line with what God wants us to do. Only in doing so will we be satisfied.

So, the Hawaiian definition of the ulu is to be possessed by the spirit so that there is an increasing presence of the Holy Spirit in the things we think, say and do. We ride a wave of concern for not only God's will for our own lives, but also for the will of God to be in all that our family, our church and our nation does.

"Loving heavenly father, help me to spend more time in your word, searching each day for that special thing that you would have me know, not that my curiosity is satisfied but that my life is changed. Forgive me when I judge others, but increase my ability to see myself before your insight, for daily that is where I am. This I pray in the name of Jesus the Christ. Amen."

BLANKET TOSS

"Then I asked, 'Who are you, Lord?' 'I am Jesus whom you are persecuting, Now get up and stand on your feet. I have appeared to you to appoint you as a servant and as a witness of what you have seen of me and what I will show you. I will rescue you from your own people and from the Gentiles. I am sending you to them to open their eyes and turn them from darkness to light, and from the power of Satan to God, so that they may receive forgiveness of sins and a place among those who are sanctified by faith in me."
Acts: 26:15-18

IT WAS AN EXCITED GROUP that grasped the blanket, stepped back and made sure that they were ready for the adventure. They would only be holding the blanket, but how they held it and how they cooperated meant safety to the man who would be tossed. They pulled tight, had a few words from the team captain and then the jumper stepped to the middle of the blanket.

A slight nod of the team captain's head and they pulled together as the jumper, who really was not doing any jumping at the moment went higher and higher. Tension showed in the faces of the blanket team and the jumper rose still higher and higher on each toss. Then he swung his arms. As he reached the highest part of the jump, more or less like a gyroscope he kept swinging his arms to maintain his stability.

It looked like fun, but this was more than a game. Higher and higher the jumper went and then he spotted the bear they were hunting. The next jump was to estimate the distance to the 'target' and then another to estimate the path that they would have to follow to creep up on the monster bear. Another jump was used to get an estimation of how much wind was blowing and from what direction. There was a final jump to make sure he could see nothing else, then he dropped to the ground, the blanket was rolled and used to tie down the sled and the group was off on the hunt.

This was not a hunt using a snow machine but one in which each of the hunters equipped with rifles stealthily walked, always keeping an iceberg, frozen in place on the sea side, between himself and the coming target. The men pulling the sled dropped behind the other hunters, for their work would begin when the bear had been killed. The marksman of the group moved off by himself while appointed persons watched a possible trail of escape for the bear, in case the marksman did not complete the kill on the first shot. The marksman fired one shot, the bear dropped and the hunt was successful.

Then came the real work as the bear was skinned and the meat was loaded on the sled. The weight of the bear was such that without separating the meat and the hide there would have been slow progress. The skin was merely dragged back to shore and would later be tanned and sold.

When the meat had been prepared and distributed to the community and the hide had been salted and processed, there was a feast. To begin the feast the hunters again grasped the blanket, a skin blanket, and as the jumper was hoisted, he shouted out, "There it is." Then on successive tosses he would describe the bear, the route that it had taken and finally the master marksman would fire his rifle in the air. The celebration continued with Eskimo dances.

Though the blanket toss is a rich cultural expression of the Eskimo, the Inupiat way of life, its real purpose is to give the hunting team an opportunity to see at a great distance. It is a quiet event when the hunt is on but its purpose is to assist the hunters to find and finally kill their quarry.

In our lead-off scripture, Paul is answering Agrippa, the king and Festus and their families. He tells of the vision that he had with Jesus the Christ and explains it in very succinct terms. It was the vision that he had followed since he met Jesus on the road to Damascus and it was the vision that he would follow for the rest of his life.

We who live a normal tunik way of life also need a vision of the future. Many things are or should be included. What is the direction that we are headed, and what is there to distract us? We must remember that normally we have 180 degrees of vision. A means of discovering this is to hold the index finger of each hand at the edge of your vision on that side. Everything behind those fingers is history, that is what is behind us-ah, but that is also important. Not only is a target an important fact of a vision, but where we started from is also important.

Our vision includes where we want to go socially, physically, morally and spiritually. Likewise our vision of the future should include those four areas. Are we happy with the social status that we have or is there some change that we would like to see? Are we physically where we want to be or are there things that we can do now to improve our physical condition? The best health is planned and worked for. Weight loss that is accomplished in a few days is usually a negative kind of weight loss. If there are other physical things that we are doing to hurt our bodies, those things should be corrected before their effect is permanent.

Morally we come from families that often have a lower than normal moral outlook on life. The use of profanity is such that it can affect our use of it and ultimately create employment problems. There is nothing legal against profanity, but many organization will not accept a person who uses it regularly. If decent language cannot be used in the work place, then the ultimate evaluation of the person is affected.

Likewise, the home affects the spiritual reality of the individual. If there is a negative spiritual relationship, that carries into all parts of your life. Again there is no legal way that it will affect a person, but it will determine what kinds of friends you have and how well you fit into a normal working relationship.

In a sense there should be a resurrection. When the jumper has given his final evaluation, the hunting party resumes the hunt as a team. There is a resurrection, in a sense, when we likewise have a vision of the future that we want and ascertain how to get to that point.

Socially, you check your friends and evaluate whether you want to keep them. Possibly there are some friends who will lead you to paths of destruction and therefore should be allowed to 'leave in peace.'

Physically, there are some things that need to be changed, resurrected. Proper eating and health habits may need to be started and incorporated into your particular life style. Exercise becomes a thing of necessity, not a thing of luxury. Regular eating and even the consultation of a health food diet can be considered.

Morally, there is still time to check up on your thoughts, actions and habits. It is hard to break a lifetime of bad habits but cutting off those things that turn people against you and your vision of the future is a necessity.

Finally, there is a need to check on your spiritual progress. The old adage for physical growth is that if you do not grow - you die. The same is true of your spiritual growth – either you grow or die. Ultimately death is a fact of life. Our tendency of course is to put it off as long as possible, but ultimately death is going to come to each of us who is alive. The only thing that cannot die is that which is dead already.

Resurrection also comes hard to those who support you, those who hold your blanket of life. Your changed lifestyle, determined by yourself and your own vision, may impinge on the lifestyles of others but there comes a time when as you have to get rid of certain friends who would invite you to join them as they jump off a cliff. Yes, you do have a right to disengage from your friends. There are others who will enhance your life, and be just as loyal or more so than the ones from whom you have chosen to distance yourself.

A successful hunt is determined by the jumper, the master hunter and all those who hold the blanket. The ultimate group in your visionary future is a God's supporting group of individuals who want the best of life for you, not in a competitive relationship but in a communal relationship with fellowship around the entire group, God and each of the team.

"Gracious God, help us as we evaluate the life that you have given us. We look to the future, here on earth and ultimately with you and would want the best of life for ourselves, our loved ones and all others. Therefore we seek the best of life for your investment in our lives. As we meet the high points in our lives, help us to see your future for us, here in the life with which we are familiar and also in your eternal purpose. This we pray in the name of Jesus the Christ, your son. Amen."

ANCIENT OR ELDERLY?

"The Lord said to Moses, 'Speak to the entire assembly of Israel!
And say to them: Be holy because I, the Lord your God, am holy.
Each of you must respect his mother and father, and you must
observe my Sabbaths. I am the Lord your God. Do not turn to
mediums or seek out spiritists, for you will be defiled by them.
I am the Lord your God. Rise in the presence of the aged, show
respect for the elderly and revere your God. I am the Lord.'"
Leviticus 19:1-3, 31-32

THE BOYS HAD BEEN OUT in their boat hunting and were told of better game, walrus, further out on the ice but the fog was rolling in. The elderly hunter suggested they return to shore, but they discounted his remarks and later had to be rescued by a helicopter.

There was an elderly man who had a problem with alcohol. The kids would laugh at him and his antics, and refused to respect him. Little did they know that their own experimenting with liquor opened them up to the same problem that he had encountered and finally conquered, and possibly would be a problem to them in the future.

One of the things that has helped the Inupiat survive in what is probably the world's worst climate is the extreme discipline that has been exercised over the youth by the elders. A young hunter does not have a written manual that he or she can consult. Those who hunt and fish in the Arctic have no time (nor warm fingers) to write manuals. They take it for granted that the youth learn from the elders. If the youth do not learn from the elders, future hunting and fishing parties are in jeopardy.

It is a truth that we all age at the same rate, every twenty-four hour period we are twenty-four hours older, but there is a difference between growing older and maturing. Those who mature learn from the elderly and that learning results in their safely reaching the age of the elderly person. It might be in the home, in the sewing of skin and material, or in the preparation of the food but learning is necessary. It may be in the operation of a boat, the handling of a weapon or the many different intricacies of hunting tracking, wind direction, or fog, the changing of off shore ice due to wind direction. It might mean the changing of storm warnings. The more skills that a youth learns, the better he is and will be at survival in the harsh climate, and fending for himself if he is alone on the wilderness.

Now it is also necessary to understand various engines, electronics and even modern phenomenon such as a Ground Position System. There is a misconception held by many youth, that a higher grade achieved in school is superior to lessons learned in the field. We might suggest that this 'learning from an elder' is also a problem in all of society. Though learning from the elderly can be a problem in other cultures, there is little room for making a mistake in the Arctic.

In one of the cities in the lower forty-eight, there is a custom of honoring the senior citizens. They are called the Honored Citizens. That acknowledges that they have been there and done that with respect to life; possibly held a job to retirement; raised a family; kept up with political trends, and volunteered for community actions. They have lived life to its fullest.

The sage is aware of the fact that if you do not read and know history, you are probably going to repeat it. The same is true with much of life as lived in the Arctic, and indeed all of the world's citizens.

In New Testament times as well as today, a Jewish lad had to pass an exam in order to become a 'man.' The exam, known as "The sons of the Covenant," and those taking the exam were required to demonstrate a thorough understanding of the book of Psalms and well as Proverbs. The tenth verse of the 111th Psalm, had to be memorized so deeply that it would spring to the lad's attention when called upon. "The fear (awe or wonder) of the Lord is the beginning of wisdom; all who follow his precepts have good understandings. To him belongs eternal praise."

When we arrived at our first church in Alaska we made it a habit to visit the elderly of the community. Many of them had been prospectors and had a knowledge of the forest around the community in which we served. They were aware of all sorts of phenomenon in the local community, the changing ice conditions in the roads, various places where there were rocks and hence a problem for navigation in the local waters, along with planting times and harvesting of local edibles. Each pastoral call was a learning experience for me. I could never have paid them what their knowledge was worth to me.

Rather than just leave this subject perhaps it is wise to suggest that we are in continually changing situations. We have people who are passing away who were the sole authorities in their particular language. This is particularly an Alaskan problem because of the various cultures in the large geographical state. Some of the languages have been carried into other parts of the United States but there is a possibility of completely losing language that was necessary to carry unique concepts that may not found in any other geographical place in the nation.

As a former pastor, I was responsible for relating concepts in English that were well defined in the Greek and Hebrew languages. Fortunately the Greeks had a culture where language and the recording of language was very important. Often a single Greek word carried a meaning that had to be explained in a paragraph in other languages. Perhaps the wisdom of youth can carry on the language of the elders.

I strongly suggest that rather than criticizing the elders, it would be wise to spend time with the elders, listening to their stories, asking questions about landmarks in the village, learning all they can, and recording the information for their children's children.

In a sense, we owe our existence to the elders who have maintained the communities in which we live. They have voted in the changes and provided the funding for new community structures. If the youth of today do not learn the history of their culture, clan or community there will be no history to convey to their own children when they reach their own ultimate maturity. It has been said that history is his-story, God's story of working with people in community.

"Loving heavenly father, We stand in awe of the wisdom of our elders and also the wisdom that you enable us to gain. Keep us humble enough to sit and listen to those who have advanced along life's road further than have we. Teach us about the world in which you have placed us and also about yourself and your love for us. For we pray in your son's name. Amen."

THE SEA WALL

"In my former book, Theophilus, I wrote about all that Jesus began
to do and to teach until the day he was taken up to heaven, after
giving instructions through the Holy Spirit to the apostles he had
chosen. After his suffering, he showed himself to these men and
gave many convincing proofs that he was alive. He appeared to them
over a period of forty days and spoke about the kingdom of God."
Acts 1:1-3

OLGOONIK IS A VILLAGE LOCATED on the Arctic Ocean, in the Bering sea.
This is an advantage as the men of the village are immediately adjacent to the
water and in a matter of minutes can launch a boat when there is a whale or
other sea animal nearby.

This also presents a problem when it comes to the warming trend in the
world, as there is an anticipation that two things will happen. The stable ice
is going to move out and that means that the polar bears will have to swim
further for feed. It also means that the ocean is encroaching on the village.

As the Northern and Southern polar ice caps melt, the weather persons and other climactic scientists tell us that water level of the ocean will rise, though with mixed amounts of water and with unconfirmed tides.

There already is a seawall located at one end of the village of Olgoonik, composed of heavy wire mesh with rocks and gravel that is supposed to keep out the ocean. For the time being it does seem to be a psychological barrier but if there is an increase in the level of the ocean the wall will have no permanent effect.

Alaska is known for its 'former' communities. The author lived for over twenty years in the Auke Village area. The Auke tribe are those Tlingit folk who lived near Auke Lake. Since the Tlingit name for 'lake' is 'Auke' The English name for Auke Lake was 'Lake Lake'. The main part of the village was at the beach site known as the Recreation Area and consisted of many houses with delineating totem poles at their corners. These are used to signify the clan of the home owners and also where folk of other similar clans in Tlingit territory were invited. Close to the author's home were two home sites that had only foundations left and the construction of a Community College destroyed them. A single totem pole indicates the site of the former village.

Kasaan was also a village of the Tlingits and was an important Indian village with many homes. These also had totem poles at the corners of the buildings designating the various clan ownership.

The village of Hoonah was originally located inside of Glacier Bay but was moved to its present site. What is more important than the geographical site are the descendants of the village, those people for whom Hoonah, or any of the other of the villages, was home. Who were the folks of the village? What cultural traditions, skills, stories and songs did they have? Are those recorded somewhere in some medium so that if the village were to be destroyed those cultural attributes to the world of knowledge would not be lost?

All of the cultures of Alaska, and that may total nine or more, were mature but growing cultures with skills, artistic and hunting abilities. The importance of this should not be lost. The artistic skills have been retained in cultural centers, and now mainly are used to sell items to visitors. Likewise, stories are told and retold through the verbal word or through native dances of the various attributes of the local cultural people.

Most of the Inupiat villages are located closely adjacent to sea water and if there is flooding due to glacial and polar ice melt they will be affected. What plans have been formulated for the possibility, that the village of Olgoonik and other costal villages will have to be moved? Hopefully, new sites will be determined close to the present sites but on ground that is elevated enough to not be flooded. There are excellent museums within the State of Alaska and fine native organizations, Alaska Federation of Natives, Alaska

Native Brotherhood and Alaska Native Sisterhood as well as cultural centers throughout the state. These can be excellent repositories of the formal history of each of the villages.

Discussion among the elders and the not-so-elders should be a conscious determination of what history the community should retain, and where the repository should be located. Verbal stories should be recorded verbally. This can be a school class project for many ambitious young people, and everything from 'creation' history to what medals the athletic teams of the community have earned should be recorded and displayed.

Alaska abounds in having many cultural modes. The history that you have lived should be recorded by those who lived it. Unless we take an active part in saving these stories they will be lost or misinterpreted. Of all the states in the United States, there are more erroneous ideas about Alaska than any other state in the union. There are also many unique features of the state, the largest in the union, with tremendous resources. Many folk believe that the next generation will "take care of our history," but the next generation does not know what you know.

We may not be able to keep the ocean from invading our land, but we can determine that the richness of who we are, where we came from and what traditions we have maintained can be preserved and understood, These things should be preserved in their native language, one that is more rich in phraseology than is modern day English. Only when the language is thoroughly understood will the people of that language really be able to express who they were, are and what hopes they had and have for the future.

The Scripture for this parable is from the beginning of the Acts of the Apostles. If Luke had not tallied, logically arranged and then recorded the events of the early church the Christian faith would have been derelict. Yes, Christ was and is the messiah, but someone needed to record the things that happened and from which we, of generations way down the historical line make a good confession of faith. Particularly valuable is the fact that Luke first wrote the gospel by his name and then recorded the acts of the early church. Theophilus was evidently his sponsor. We know nothing more about him except that without him the world might never have known the son of God, who is ultimately the savior of the world.

"Father God, father of all of us regardless of culture and language, help and inspire us to complete the living of our lives by recording that which we did, thought and acted during our time on the planet earth. We thank you for your son who was raised a Hebrew, whose life was recorded in Greek and whose life is now translated into all the languages of the world. In his name we pray. Amen."

SINGING

"About midnight Paul and Silas were praying and singing hymns
to God, and the other prisoners were listening to them. Suddenly
there was such a violent earthquake that the foundations of the
prison were shaken. At once all the prison doors flew open, and
everybody's chains came loose. The jailer woke up, and when
he saw the prison doors open, he drew his sword and was about
to kill himself because he thought the prisoners had escaped.
But Paul shouted, 'Don't harm yourself! We are all here!'"
Acts 16:25-28

IT WAS WARM IN THE sanctuary and some had great difficulty keeping their
eyes open, but the benediction was a lusty hymn and the glazed donuts were
appreciated in the social hall. The chairs were arranged as though a meeting
was to take place and with donuts in hand the folks seated themselves. After
a short prayer the people pulled out the Inupiat song books and sang from
number one. The microphones were in order, tested to make sure that the
volumes were compatible and the announcer spoke into the pulpit mike: "We
welcome you to our service of singing. From Kaktovik to Anaktuvik Pass
to the Chukchi Sea, we bring you greetings from the Utkeagvik church in
Barrow, we are all united in song."

Meanwhile there was a man furiously writing at the radio. He would
then hand a paper to the choir director and the hymn would be announced,
The announcer then would say, "From Marion Agaruk to the Ipalook family
camped for the night along the Colville River and from Boots to Candy
Ahmaogak in Nuiqsut."

The gathered choir would then sing all the stanzas of the hymn and
everyone on the North Slope would be not only entertained but also brought
closer together by the singing over the radio network. The warm rays of
fellowship crisscrossed the Northern part of the State of Alaska as dedications
continued until the early hours of Monday morning.

How Great Thou Art!

Carl Boberg
English Trans. by Stuart K. Hine
Iñupiat Tr. by Martha N. Aiken

Swedish Melody

1. A - ta - niiq God, a - liu - ġu - ti - gi - git - ka, i - sum - ma - ti - gi - git - ka sa - vaa - tin; Uv - lu - ġiat - tauq, kal - lug - lu ak - sra - lik - tuaq, suaŋ - ŋa - tin nu - na - mi ma - niuq - tuaq - taak.

2. Na - paaq - tu - ti - gun pi - sua - ġa - lua - qa - ma, tu - saġ - naq - tut tiŋ - miaġ - ruich a - tuq - tuat; Iġ - ġi - miḷ - ḷu tau - tuak - srat a - liug - naq - tut, tusaav - lu - gu - lu kuu - ġuq maq - sra - luk - tuaq.

3. Isum - ma - ti - gi - gi - ga God tili - raa iġ - ñi, tu - qu - taut - quv - lu - gu aŋar - rau - ra - mi; Ti - gu - miaġ - miv - lu - gich uqu - maiḷ - ḷi - raat - ka, tu - qu - tau - ruq piḷuu - tai - ġiaq - saq - ḷu - ŋa.

4. Christ qai - ñiaq - tuq ni - paq - pau - ti - qaġ - lu - ni, ag - gi - sik - pa - ŋa quvia - sug - niaq - tu - ŋa; Pun - niaq - tu - ŋa, i - laa nan - ġaġ - lu - gu - lu, uqal - lag - lu - ŋa, "God - iiŋ kama - naq - tu - tin"!

96

How Great Thou Art

The singing would continue until the last request had been sung, and there was a short Benediction. The Barrow people would feel the thrill of satisfaction as they had spent the entire evening joining people thousands of miles apart with their singing. And in the lonely camps you could have heard the folks also singing along. It was not necessary to have accompaniment as everyone knew the songs and could easily drop into their accepted part. Often if there were few basses, the tenors would drop down to strengthen the section. Jokingly one mentioned that if he had the equipment he could sing all four parts of the songs just by himself through re-recording.

One of the main things in bringing the Inupiat folk together is the singing of their favorite hymns in their own language. One person would start the song, sort of a pitch pipe person and the rest would join in with some of the most wonderful harmony that anyone has ever known.

Though the folk of the Arctic Slope are separated by thousands of miles of distance, experiences, communities and even more fish and hunting camps, the Sunday evening singing has brought them all close. There are almost no messages because everyone is listening and few people want to gossip with hundreds of others listening in, but occasionally one slips in. There is nothing in the way of advertising, and no one is urging you to attend this or that church.

The purpose is fellowship and though some denominations have come in and split families apart, the singing brings folks together. No one is trying to outdo anyone else and in reality it is just a time of musical fellowship. Often the same song is sung several times in a particular evening because the radio operator, though taking as many calls as possible and as fast as possible, keeps busy handing the lead slips of the music. Occasionally the director has a difficulty with some radio reception, but there is a close feeling of fellowship on the slope.

One of the main worries as the Inupiat culture comes in contact with the sophisticated tunik culture is that the young people, often with ear phones glued to their ears, are not learning the songs in Inupiat from the elders and therefore are being separated from their other friends. Most of those who attend no longer need songbooks as they have memorized the songs.

To a great extent, the theology of the Inupiat folk comes from their singing, so some of the newer songs that do not carry deep theology are not acceptable to the singers. Church services are non-existent in the isolation of summer hunting and fishing camps but this time of singing brings far flung families into closer relationship with each other and with God.

There is a unifying force involved in singing. You and I may be of completely different denominations and theological viewpoints but when we sing together to praise God, those differences are forgotten.

There is no stronger praise to God than a group of people singing "How Great Thou Art" in Korean, English, Yupic, Tlingit, Hawaiian and Inupiat. Maybe if people sang more and argued less there would be a stronger presence of people worshiping God. I still remember the song sung in my home church, "I know whom I have believed and am persuaded that he is able to keep that which I've committed unto him against that day." It is scripture - but it is also song and praise. May God bless us all as we praise him together, uniting not only ourselves with God but ourselves with each other in like congregations and also in the love of the church.

Our Scripture passage tells of Paul and Silas who were imprisoned in the town of Philippi and at midnight, yes, from memory, they were singing songs and praying. As a result of a God inspired earthquake they were freed. May God feel the strength that we have as we sing to him.

"Gracious God, whether we harmonize, vocalize or just sing by ourselves we do sing to you. May our love to you be expressed not in the perfection of the sound but in the fervor of the singing as we come into your presence. Help us to be honest as we place ourselves in praise of you, the Lord of the universe. This we pray in the name of Jesus the Christ. Amen."

FOG

"Do not let your hearts be troubled. Trust in God; trust also in me. In my Father's house are many rooms; if it were not so, I would have told you. I am going there to prepare a place for you. And if I go and prepare a place for you, I will come back and take you to be with me that you also may be where I am. You know the way to the place where I am going. Thomas said to him 'Lord, we don't know where you are going, so how can we know the way?' Jesus answered, 'I am the way and the truth and the life. No one comes to the Father except through me. If you really knew me, you would know my Father as well. From now on, you do know him and have seen him.'"
John 14:1-7

ONE OF THE FACTS ABOUT the Northern Coast of Alaska is FOG. It makes no difference whether you are flying, traveling in a boat, using a snow machine, or an All Terrain Vehicle Fog, fog, fog is something that you see all the time. It can be a beautiful day with the sun (not warmly) shining on the entire North Coast and fog will come creeping in. You can be on an ice flow with a bearded walrus in your sights and then fog can come in so that you can't see how to get to the animal after you shoot him.

You can leave Barrow on a plane for the short 100 mile trip to Olgoonik and by the time you are half way to your destination the fog has come in. You may be going the other direction and again the fog comes in forcing you to find an alternate field on which to land.

With the Beaufort Sea meeting the Chukchi Sea, ice bergs everywhere, a melting tundra and lots of moisture, and lots of fog is a distinct reality.

The fog itself cannot hurt you, for we breathe fog and it presents no problem. The problem is that fog prevents our seeing anything else but the fog. We can be sure of a particular course as we follow the magnetic forces of the compass, but we have no visual way of knowing whether or not there is something in the way, like a mountain or some other kind of hindrance.

Likewise, flying can be beautiful but the minute the ground is obscured by the fog you have a problem, and you can't stay up in the air forever. And of course there is also ice fog, where the particles of fog are frozen.

We recall flying into Fairbanks, yet we could not see the city nor the airport. Fortunately the pilot knew more than did we and by following a particular set of landmarks, we came over the field and landed on the strip, but then had to be guided with a pilot car to the terminal. With the exhausts of the automobiles along with other heating units, the ice fog was only over part of the city, but that was the part that we wanted to visit.

So the more I think about fog the more I wonder whether or not there is some fog in my own life that keeps me from seeing things as they really are. Is my genetic background, the way that I have been taught and the reasoning system that I use so fogged up that I cannot see things as reality- or possibly I do see things as reality.

I am not the only citizen to walk the planet earth, but I am a citizen of the earth and I am here on earth right now in the year 2008. I live in a country that allows me to think as I please and really has only a few simple rules to assist me in getting along with my fellow citizens. I agree to drive on the right-hand side of the road, although I will drive on the left-hand side when I move into countries where that is the way of driving. I can't blame the other drivers if I decide to exercise my freedom by driving on the wrong side of the road .

I have been trained to think of the other people that share the earth with me. It is my intent to understand those who have been raised under differing systems of education, personal privilege and different morals. Though I may understand why they live by different rules, I accept the fact that when they move into the country that I call my own, of which I am a part, but not an owner, then it is up to them to live by the same rules that I live by. Just because you have the right to drive on the left-hand side of the road in your own country does not mean that you have the right to drive on the left-hand side of the road in the United States.

If your religion says that you can do various things, such as having multiple wives or forcing people to do things that I consider unjust, and if you live in my country either you change the way you do things or you move back to the country from which you came. After all, if I moved into the country from which you came I would have to live by the rules of your country. If I didn't then I would be in trouble or I would have to leave.

I think that every citizen of the earth has the right to freely determine who and where he wants to be, and what he or she wants to do with his or her life. But we should admit that there are other kinds of fog, a mind set that keeps us from seeing things as they really are.

At the time of this writing we are involved in a presidential campaign. There are those who are embedded in a fog of political affiliation, who can see nothing wrong with their own candidate but can find many things wrong with the other opposing candidate. It seems that no amount of fact can change the fog that surrounds the other person, though of course I can see the sunlight that surrounds my choice.

There are some involved in the fog of sports. Their year is determined not by the seasons of the year but by the dominant sport whether it is football, baseball, basketball, soccer, tennis, golf or some other sport. No amount of drugs taken, or errors made or anything else can change their way of looking at things. The heros are the athletes and the products that the athletes use, or the political leanings that the athletes have guide them in their thinking. To them everything is sports, even to complaining that the sports page should be the first page of every paper or magazine.

There are others who have a fog of money. Again their entire focus is money and everything is determined by how much they can gain and how little they can spend. One of their chief recreations, if you can call it that, is to make money by gambling. There the idea is to get a lot by giving a little, though they must admit that they are giving much more than they are getting.

But money, money, money is everything and the business page with the stock market listings should be the first page in the paper and the first news report of the day, particularly when the stock market has already opened by the time we wake up. There is a fog of money that they cannot penetrate and money is all they can see in all of their actions and relationships.

I owned a car that had fog lights. These light were mounted low at the front of the car and were deliberately aimed lower than the usual beams of lights. When I drove with the fog lights I could actually see more because the cone of light was lower to the ground, although the fog was still there.

So I propose that we have a fog light which allows us to see things as they really are and also helps us get through the fog that we may not realize that we have. This fog light is Jesus the Christ. You could have guessed it when you read the Scripture at the beginning of this parable. He has been the way to God even before he came to the planet earth. As the Scripture says, if you see him you have seen God and you know what God wants you to do.

Notice that I said that the fog lights point down, down to the basics. And that basic is that God loves you, created you and wants you to love him. Sure, it is hard loving someone you don't know so you get to know him better and that love, a giving kind of love, grows so that it becomes more fun to follow the way of Jesus the Christ. With the Fatherhood Of God {FOG} you find that the obstacles are really challenges, that the mountains that seem to block your way really have paths up and through them or around them. Your life becomes one of growth and joy in the accomplishing of God's will for you.

But let me add one short note. With satellites we now have what is known as a GPS, or Ground Positioning System. With the small hand held device picking up sensitivity from satellites, you can tell exactly where on the planet earth you are. There is a lot of fog in the world, whether it be physical, mental or spiritual. When **G**od's love in the **P**resence of the **S**avior is in your life there is no stumbling (challenging) situation that can overcome you.

"Father, and I say it with a sense of awe and also love, I thank you that your son reveals as much as we need to know, now, of who you really are. We look forward to a newer relationship, a closer walking and a total trusting of our lives to your will. Keep us on the path with Jesus as our brother-savior as we walk the earth at your will, in Jesus name we pray. Amen."

THE SILENT SAINT

"Therefore put on the full armor of God, so that when the day
of evil comes, you may be able to stand your ground, and after
you have done everything, to stand. Stand firm, then with the
belt of truth buckled around your waist, with the breastplate of
righteousness in place, and with your feet fitted with the readiness
that comes from the gospel of peace. In addition to all this, take up
the shield of faith, with which you can extinguish all the flaming
arrows of the evil one. Take the helmet of salvation and the sword
of the Spirit, which is the word of God and pray in the spirit on
all occasions with all kinds of prayers and requests. With this in
mind, be alert and always keep on praying for all the saints."
Ephesians 6:13-18

IN CHECKING MY COPY OF the New Columbia Encyclopedia, I find that over
one hundred saints are listed, all beginning with a capital "S". I then find that
the Bible is also full of saints, but not one of them has a capital "s." Rather
they are listed and described in lower case letters.

Then to make sure that I know what I am dealing with I find in my
Random House Webster's College Dictionary that a saint is:
1. A person of exceptional holiness, formally recognized by the Christian
   Church (Roman Catholic) especially by canonization.
2. A person of great virtue or benevolence.
3. A founder or patron.
4. A member of any of various Christian groups.

So I conclude that a saint is capitalized in the Roman Catholic denomination
of the Christian Church, but that every member of a Protestant Christian
Church is a saint, albeit the Protestant saints are never capitalized.

As I think of the Olgoonik Church I think of many who are saints.
There are lay folk who have been loyal to the church over many years and,
of course, the pastors. Names of the pastors that come to mind are Dr. Rev.
Henry Griests who helped organize the congregation June 24, 1923 and a
succession of persons: Roy Ahmaogak, Samuel Simmonds, Percy Ipalook, the
Lou Graftons, Mrs. Patricia Berg and Roger Kemp.

There are many lay folk who have been loyal over the years but there is another saint whom many forget, and that was Dr. J. Earl Jackman. Dr. Jackman was the Board of National Missions representative who was secretary for and maintained the work in Alaska. Until the presbyteries were really organized he was responsible for hiring (and firing?) those who came to serve as pastors.

He would leave New York (475 Riverside Drive) with galoshes and a raincoat and end up with a parka and mukluks while trying to keep a schedule, getting from one remote Alaskan outpost to another. It was not uncommon for him to be caught doing the supper dishes prior to an evening meeting, while the missionary wife put the kids to bed.

He had a high standard for the pastors, which included regular calling on the members of the congregation, not just those who were sick or dying. These calls had to be recorded each month. Then he enforced a policy of non-smoking, non-drinking of alcoholic beverages, Biblically based preaching and an involvement in the community. He emphasized preparation for sermons and participation in other activities of the churches.

Another example of his sainthood was at the Board meetings in New York when funds were going to be allocated to all sorts of projects. It was his strong feeling that such funds be allocated to the churches of Alaska, and Olgoonik was one of these churches.

He was short of stature and some felt that because of his size he 'fought harder' for the causes in which he believed. Those were the individual Sunday School missions as well as the remote Alaskan Churches. His little black book contained the necessary information so that when called upon, he could accurately report on the needs of the Alaskan, and that included Olgoonik Presbyterian churches.

Where Dr. Sheldon Jackson was a primary instigator and motivator for many mission activities, Dr. Jackman was a continual supporter of the work in Alaska. Many missions would have failed had it not been for Dr. Jackman's careful attention, some call it excessively proper relationships with the churches and pastors.

He kept an accurate record of the needs, whether expressed or not, of the various pastors and through the years worked to strengthen the Presbyteries so that they could become self-determining and self-supporting. To do this he spoke at churches on his way to and from Alaska and in New York so that support was sufficient until those that would become self supporting attained that status.

Possibly the most difficult of his many chores was to quietly refrain when it came time to "pass the baton" to the next administrative style, recognizing that he was part of a transition that was necessary for the congregation to grow.

Every pastor knows that such action is difficult, but it is Jesus Christ who is the Lord of the Church, not the former pastor, or the former administrator. With Dr. Jackman this was a continuing process as more and more the Presbytery of Yukon and the Presbytery of Alaska became self-determining judicatories.

Only as one looks back from the perspective of history does one see the leadership that was involved in the establishment of Presbyterian Mission in Alaska. The buildings as well as the mission were strong and capable of long term mission. In the Presbyterian form of government there was and is a need for the lay persons of the local churches as well as of the geographical area to take a position of leadership. This is seen to be more difficult as the cultural modes of the people served were not always consistent with the representative needs of the denomination, many leaders being not the high caste persons of the cultural group.

We need to be aware of the fact that each person making a declaration of Faith in Jesus Christ as the Son of God is acting in the personage of a saint of the church. Some are shown in actual leadership and others are behind the scenes giving financially anonymously, serving in ways that do not draw attention to their actions or persona, and affecting the life of the church in a positive way. In most cases their denominational background or inheritance does not affect their sainthood. Indeed often the sainthood comes through regardless of the denominational mold.

We might also mention that those who have been canonized, according to their denominational mold still are saints as God sees their service to the church and mankind.

"Gracious father of us all, we seek in humility to be the persons you would wish us to be, filling that place in the Kingdom of God that is reserved for the workers. We ask for wisdom to see the places where we should present ourselves, and we ask for the strength and wisdom to fulfil the position that you have for us. May your will be done in all that we do. This we pray in the name of Jesus the Christ who came as our messiah and savior. Amen."

THE SHAMAN

"When Abram was ninety-nine years old, the Lord appeared to him
and said, 'I am God Almighty; walk before me and be blameless.
I will confirm my covenant between me and you and will greatly
increase your numbers.' Abram fell face down, and God said to him,
'As for me, this is my covenant with you. You will be the father of
many nations. No longer will you be called Abram; your name will
be Abraham, for I have made you a father of many nations.'"
Genesis 17:1-5

THE SHAMAN IN INUPIAT CULTURE has often been maligned by the English
word for the individual, namely Witch Doctor. Perhaps a better way to define
the shaman is by describing his duties within the culture of his times. Among
other things he was:

A <u>medical doctor</u> prescribing herbs and other medicines that were needed
for the healing of individuals. This often meant that he picked and stored
the herbs until such time as they were needed. His home usually was not as
accessible as the homes in the rest of the village.

A <u>psychologist</u> who brought either training or common sense to situations
when calm and a third person was needed to bring together estranged
individuals. In a close isolated village, such a person held the families together,
not only protecting the families but the entire village by determining when
an individual or situation was not good for the community.

An <u>historian</u>, who heard and remembered the stories of the past of the
village and who could be called upon to repeat those stories. This gave the
village not only an annual record, but a record into their past.

A <u>genealogist</u> who knew the various families of the village and could
relate how they were tied together through direct relationships or marriage
relationships. In villages where grandchildren often were named for
grandparents, such an individual brought a sense of timeliness and timelessness
to a people whose main purpose was self-survival.

A <u>weather prognosticator</u>, who was so aware of the weather that he could
relate what to expect when various patterns of weather seemed to prevail.
Though you might know about weather, it was always good to check with

the shaman to make sure you were right. If there was a difference, then best to listen to him.

A teacher, though most teaching was done in the local home with girls being taught the duties and functioning of women in the community and the boys being taught the manly things that were necessary for survival. Still, someone had to be able to teach all other subjects, boundaries of the village and hunting and fishing areas, taboos, the sharpening of realized skills of the individual members of the village and the shaman was that teacher. Ultimately he had to pass on his knowledge.

A spiritualist, responsible to assuage the spirits of animals killed for sustenance and for other spirits believed to be transferred though the normal hunting. The beginnings of the village came from someone, somewhere, and those spirits of those people had to be understood, and rearranged in an order that was understandable. There was also a problem between good and evil and often the shaman, because he could tell the difference, had an extreme amount of power, that he could use for either evil or good causes. Reading was not an art because you had nothing to read and there was no room in the village for such things as books so memorization was a necessity.

A judge, for in many cases there were differences between individuals or families, and the shaman was as 'neutral' a person as they could find, with no written law to follow but at the same time a need for common sense.

A magician, where magic was used not only for healing, but also was incorporated into his own persona. Because he could produce magic and others couldn't, he was considered a very special person.

An astronomer, who understood not only the seasons of the year but also the functioning of the stars and the moon. He not only knew about the stars but could also use them to guide others physically on the seas and on land, as well as spiritually through the realms of eternity.

A local artist, whose art consisted of pictures on hide, or carving of ivory or bone, or as arranging of articles in an artistic mode.

An entertainer, and sometimes the leader of the music to which the people danced. The music might only be the beat of a drum along with singing or chanting, but it was the Shaman's responsibility to pass the chants down to successive generations, even if the shaman was tone deaf. Often the dances interpreted local customs or historical events and therefore were necessary for teaching.

A politician, who was the individual who negotiated with other communities to make sure that the entire structure of society was maintained, not only internally but between various villages, determining boundaries for hunting and fishing areas, and other infractions of culture.

Everything else, for some things were not included in the list, but if anything was in question in the community the shaman was consulted and became an immediate expert.

Because he fulfilled so many roles, the shaman was more or less a protected individual. Whaling, hunting and fishing were dangerous industries and often a boat with seven or eight men of the village could be lost. Though they were never replaced, at least the village did continue. Hence, the shaman was seldom on a hunt. His loss was irreplaceable and when he knew or felt that he was going to die, prognosticating his own death, it was necessary to train another shaman or shamans to pick up the knowledge that he had for use in the village in the future. Normally he was the one to choose the future shaman, this decision not being left up to the community. The job was often hereditary, but if he had no immediate family then it was his responsibility to choose a person from one of the village families. This meant separating that person from the regular village activities.

As is true in all societies, an individual with such powers was often feared or the target of jealousy. It was also true that if anything that went wrong in the community, on a hunt, in a marriage or with respect to relationships to others in the community, it was automatically the fault of the shaman. In a later culture, an "act of God" was always laid at the feet of the shaman, when often he had nothing that he could do to ameliorate the situation.

Because of his situation, he could also be the loneliest individual in the village, because many feared being closely associated to him. Of course he was a member of a family unit of the community and had those normal relationships.

As other cultures came into the geographical area of the Inupiat the powers of the shaman were taken over by others with different training. His position and power decreased when the community had less and less need of him. Eventually the shaman was not needed at all.

Such individuals had to be respected as so much of the social life of the community depended upon their abilities and their willingness to serve the community. Later as Christian pastors and doctors came into the area, the powers of the shaman were often felt to be those powers of the doctors and spiritual leaders. Slowly education has eased the shaman into a necessity of antiquity, while the new leaders have had to assume more than their abilities could provide.

In a sense Abram, on his journey to the promised land with everything that he owned and his immediate family, assumed the power of the shaman for the Israelites. The only difference, found in the scripture at the beginning of this parable, was that he moved at the instigation of God toward his eternal purpose of bringing peace to all nations. New laws would be assumed and new concerns met. Ultimately God would accomplish a new relationship with the people of the earth through Abraham. These people are from all nations, all races, all tribes and are defined as individuals who on faith have accepted God at his word. The process is still in progress.

"Gracious God, you unite us not only geographically with other cultures of the world but also with their histories of cultures, and in the world. We admire your wisdom as you have brought knowledge of yourself and your world to mankind. Help us to understand that which we need to know to honor and glorify you, not only in worship but also in our daily activities as we live with one another. In your son's name we pray. Amen."

THE HUNT

"They devoted themselves to the apostles' teaching and to the
fellowship, to the breaking of bread and to prayer. Everyone
was filled with awe, and many wonders and miraculous signs
were done by the apostles. All the believers were together and
had everything in common. Selling their possessions and goods,
they gave to anyone as he had need. Every day they continued
to meet together in the temple courts. They broke bread in their
homes and ate together with glad and sincere hearts, praising
God and enjoying the favor of all the people. And the Lord
added to their number daily those who were being saved."
Acts 2:42-47

HUNTING IN NORTH SLOPE ALASKA is not a sport. No one buys expensive
clothes from some supplier in Seattle, but rather they use their Eskimo skins
and furs to keep warm. There is no thought that they are looking for the
largest of animals in any specific classification. They are hunting meat and
fur and ivory and it is those three found on an animal that drives the hunter
to risk his life in what even he considers miserable weather. If the miserable
weather brings the animal close enough to shoot, then it is good weather.

The Inupiat hunter of 2008 faces many obstacles. First is the warming
trend creating differing hunting conditions. Warm weather means that the
ice is not solid and where the hunter used to hunt on the ice it is no longer
always safe to do so. Likewise the warming trend means that the animals
being hunted change some of their environment. Whether they are land
animals that move away from their traditional grounds, or sea-born animals
that are venturing further north, there are new problems in the old patterns
of hunting.

There is also the trend to put some of the animals on the endangered,
species list, and are no longer legal to hunt. Battles over the endangerment
of polar bears, between environmentalists and subsistence hunters and sport
hunters are continuing. Some felt that hunting of the polar bear should be
opened to commercial hunting at all times and others felt that all hunting,

subsistence as well as commercial hunting should be abolished. As northern Canada has the same animals, the discussion has become international.

There has been an ongoing battle between subsistence whaling, particularly of the Alaskan villages, and the Japanese whalers who say that they are whaling under the guise of "study," but so far no study has been forthcoming, and they sell the whales commercially.

With the warming trends that are occurring, there are possibilities that the habits of the various kinds of whales are changing. There are fifteen species of whales found in different parts of Alaska. These are: beluga, Bering Sea beaked, blue, bowhead, fin, giant bottlenose, goose-beaked, gray, humpback, killer, minke, narwhal, right, sei and sperm. They are divided into two classifications: those that have baleen, and feed on krill and fish, and the others that are toothed whales and hunt other marine animals like seal and porpoise.

Walrus is a multi-product animal. It's hide is used for skin boats, the tusks are used for ivory that can be artistically carved, the intestines are used to make rain gear, and the meat is food for the natives. The walrus also eats seals.

The seals seem to be the basic diet of most of Alaska's mammals. The walrus thrive on it and the polar bears prefer seal. A study has shown that seals make air holes in the ice so that they can breathe, but the Polar bears wait by these holes for the seals to appear. Researchers found that the seal can see the black nose of the polar bear, so the polar bears now cover their nose with their front paws. The seals are then grabbed when they come to the surface.

The Pacific bearded seal is the one most hunted by the hunters of Olgoonik. The males can sometimes weigh as much as 750 pounds in the winter. The meat is called oogruk and is the staple of the Eskimo cuisine. Harbor seals and also sea lions are prized but seldom travel north of the Pribilof Islands.

Reindeer were introduced to Alaska by Dr. Sheldon Jackson and now there are many wild herds that move from the Southern range to the Northern range, coming through the passes such as at Anaktuvik Pass (Anaktuvik meaning 'reindeer droppings') Caribou, have wide hoofs that make it possible to travel over summer-time moss and winter snow.

One means of hunting is by trapping smaller animals. Trap lines can be dangerous to lynx, rabbits, foxes. Minks, wolverines and martens, that are white-in-winter and brown-in-summer. Most trap lines are worked in the winter when the weather keeps the Eskimo hunter out of the distant wilderness. The Eskimo hunter also hunts ducks divided into land ducks and also water ducks. The difference is that water ducks are year round while the land ducks move in and out with the seasons.

There comes a time when the Eskimo hunter feels that it is time to stop. For the whaler it means pulling his boat way up on the beach and turning it over for the rest of the season. For the land hunter it means observing a time of rest so that the seasons can change. At such a time an *apuk* is held. This means that everyone in town comes in pick up trucks and ATVs with plastic bags (for carrying home parts of the meat) and there is a feast.

The average Olgoonik home is too small for large groups of people. The bigger the home the more you have to heat, so there are chairs arranged for the leaders or the elders of the family, but the rest of the folk are given the food that they would normally have at the *apuk,* (muktuk, duck soup, fermented muktuk, whale meat, fruit and bread*)* and it is taken home.

Possibly no other community in the world is as generous as the Eskimo community in sharing what they have with everyone around them. They are truly a community. The time is coming, nay, is way past when the world needs to see itself as a community. Only as we see ourselves as some great family can we truly accept the fact that God is our Father, Jesus the Christ is his Son and our Savior, and we are all truly brothers and sisters.

"Forgive us, Father God, for the inclination that we have to separate ourselves from all 'others' and cling only to all who are like us. May we truly embody in our lives the concept of total family-hood as expressed in our prayer, 'Our Father who art in heaven, hallowed by they name. Thy kingdom come, thy will be done on earth as it is in heaven. Give us this day our daily bread and forgive us our sins as we forgive those who sin against us. Lead us not into temptation but deliver us from evil for thine is the kingdom, and the power and the glory for ever. Amen.'"

I HAVE A DREAM

"And afterward, I will pour out my Spirit on all people. Your sons and daughters will prophesy, your old men will dream dreams, and your young men will see visions. Even on my servants, both men and women, I will pour out my Spirit in those days. I will show wonders in the heavens and on the earth, blood and fire and billows of smoke."
Joel 2:28-30

THERE ARE MANY WHO CLAIM to have dreams as did Joel. The dream meant much to him, and also has become important to those who care to read the entire passage. The verses above are just a short part. I know how he dreamed, and I also have a dream.

Now I did not say that I had a dream, as though it was something that is all finished now that I am awake. No, rather I have a dream, and it is a dream now. It is not a sleeping dream, combining things that my mind has picked up over the 80% of a century that I have lived. There are always those who want to know what I dreamed so that they can see if they are part of it. Well, those dreams are very private things and I intend to keep them that way,

We are entering a distinct period in the life of our nation. We have been living with Baby Boomers for the last fifty years. They were born at the end of World War Two and the philosophers and all the rest can tell us why, but they have gone through a school system that had to be enlarged for them. Then there had to be enough jobs to keep them all busy and there had to be all sorts of fads to keep them happy. We changed music styles, we changed humor, we even tried to balance the world by sending a couple of them to the moon. They have added much to our American dream.

But I have a dream

Now the Boomers are retiring, folding up their work plans and hoping to have all the things that they felt they did not get, but which they feel they deserved. At the same time there were many boomer pastors, both female and male. They have served well in the church, and they have been responsible for many large congregations. In some cases, those churches have more folks attending worship than there is population in some of our small Alaskan towns. That is not to say that the folk joined the churches, but they did attend.

The boomer pastors have served them well, often in a grandiose style. Now the boomer pastors are retiring.

But I have a dream.

To a great extent the boomer pastors have become specialists in sermon preparation and preaching, in Christian Education of Children and in worship experiences where the new style of music was projected on screens because it probably would not be around long enough to get printed in a book. They are specialists in using the combos, including guitars, drums and any other instruments that they could find with a strong beat, and often a rather loud microphone.

They are specialists with youth, with lots of events, trips to mission stations and projects around their own towns.

But I have a dream

The boomer pastors are now retiring. Some are retiring as soon as they can, soon after the age of sixty. They are looking forward to taking some of the cruises that their parents have been taking, playing golf eight hours a day whether it is rainy or shiny. Some have hobbies they want to follow, or possibly even a second, or would it be a third career. They have had good success in their ministries and the Lord has said, "Well done thou good and faithful servants. You have worked hard, enter into the presence of the Lord," not that they were not there anyway.

But, I have a dream.

The many baby boomer pastors look forward to getting the well-deserved retirement package that they worked for all their lives. In some cases it was a denominational retirement package and in other cases they decided to have a 401 (k) retirement package, Perhaps there were some investments that they wisely put away so that they are financially set up for retirement. Most have pension plans that take into consideration their health needs for the rest of their lives.

But, I have a dream

The boomer's children are now all raised. Oh, yes, some of them came back home for all sorts of good reasons, whether they were not quite settled and needed time to think, or because of frustration with jobs. Perhaps they needed to rest financially easy for a few years and found that home was the best place to relax, rethink and restart their lives. Some came home because mom's cookies were better than Girl Scout Cookies and also much more plentiful.

But, I have a dream

And that dream is that those who have served well, so well that they aught not to stop as long as they still have their health, financial health, mental health and spiritual health will accept more challenges. And while they have their health that possibly there is still another challenge which can come to them because:

I have a dream.

That those who have served well will consider working with small, isolated groups of Christians who also have a dream of some day having a pastor just their own, or who is not tied to a church that rewards you with glittering gifts because you attend and bring a neighbor three weeks in a row. They do not want to continually hear how much they are sinners, and that an angry God will condemn them and the life style that they are living. No:

I have a dream

That you, the reader, might consider that all those things that you have read in this book up to this point, might point to you the need for your additional service in a remote village in Alaska. You will not compare the size of your congregation with the congregation in the next village, for size is not that important. It was the quality of Jesus the Christ's life that was important, not the quantity of years that he ministered.

He had a dream

That those who had been successful in other endeavors would pick up the dream that he had of a world reconciled to God the Father through the Jesus Christ the son. When his life on earth was completed, the disciples attached to that dream and then sort of exploded by going into all the world. At first it was a quiet explosion, but as time went on they kept hearing that others had made a difference in the areas to which they went and then it dawned on each of them that they had answered the call of Jesus Christ to serve. Indeed they had served, and that they were not alone, for Jesus the Christ went with them and the Holy Spirit would do all sorts of things, as long as the believer kept moving. And the fun of ministry is that wherever you turn there is something new and grand and glorious that you never thought was possible because

You had a dream.

And you can fulfil your dream for the next few years, taken care of by the denomination that took care of you, faithful to the call that Christ issued to you many years ago, a call without termination, that people might join in fellowship with a new concept of peace that might begin in a remote, culturally distinct, but geographically isolated village, that sits on top of countless energy resources that the world wants. And God still has wonderful things that need to be done, that can be done by an experienced pastor and his or her spouse. Who knows but that heaven is not a resting place but a place where God gives us further challenges and the reason he does is because we proved that we could handle them here on earth. The Kingdom of God might come on earth, right here, right now because,

You had a dream.

"Gracious God help us in our dreaming that we might put deeds and commitment together to fulfill and fill full your dream for all mankind that, 'Your kingdom will come, your will be done on earth as it is in heaven.' Amen."

SCRIPTURE REFERENCE

SCRIPTURE	CHAPTER
Genesis 1:26-28	EVEN THE WHALES OBEY
Genesis 12:1-4	OLGOONIK INTERNATIONAL RACEWAY
Genesis 17:1-5	THE SHAMAN
Leviticus 19:1-3, 31-32	ANCIENT OR ELDERLY?
Psalm 1:1-3	I THINK THAT I SHALL NEVER SEE, A TREE
Psalm 49:16-18	WANTED: A PASTOR
Psalm 84:1-3	THE CENTER OF OLGOONIK
Psalm 116:15-19	EMPTY PILINGS
Proverbs 1:2-5	CELL PHONE SILLINESS CEASES
Proverbs 1:8-12	MOSQUITOS
Ecclesiastes 5:18-20	ESKIMO LABOR
Daniel 3:16-18	THE LONGEST DAY OF THE YEAR
Jonah 3:1, 2, 5, 10	WHALING CAPTAIN
Joel 2:28-30	I HAVE A DREAM
Matthew 6:9-15	FATHER'S DAY IN OLGOONIK
Matthew 16:1-4	WEATHER - WEATHER - WEATHER
Matthew 25:34-40	TANIK
Matthew 28:16-20	SEALSKIN WALLETS
Mark 3:31-35	HOW DRY I AM
Mark 6:38-44	THE SMALL CHURCH AS JSF
John 14:1-4	THE IGLOO
John 14:1-7	FOG
Acts l:1-3	THE SEA WALL
Acts 2:42-47	THE HUNT

Acts 13:1-3	AND WHOSE TRIP ARE YOU ON?
Acts 16:25-28	SINGING
Acts 16:6-10	NOT YET, SON
Acts 26:15-18	BLANKET TOSS
Romans 8:35,37-39	THE CAKE WALK
I Corinthians 3:10-13	MY LIFE AS A GOPHER
Ephesians 6:13-18	THE SILENT SAINT
Philippians 4:21-23	LIVING TRANSPARENTLY
I Timothy 1:3-7	ROTTEN ICE THEOLOGY
Hebrews 4:12-13	ULU
Hebrews 13:14-18a	OLGOONIK, THE FAVORED CITY
Revelation 22:18,19	PLANES WITH SHOES